Real Life Parenting

of
Kids with Diabetes

Virginia Nasmyth Loy

American
Diabetes
Association.
Cure • Care • Commitment℠

Director, Book Publishing, John Fedor; *Book Acquisitions and Editor*, Sherrye L. Landrum; *Production Manager*, Peggy M. Rote; *Composition*, Circle Graphics, Inc.; *Cover Design*, VC Graphics Design Studio; *Printer*, Port City Press

Printed in the United States of America
1 3 5 7 9 10 8 6 4 2

The suggestions and information contained in this publication are generally consistent with the *Clinical Practice Recommendations* and other policies of the American Diabetes Association, but they do not represent the policy or position of the Association or any of its boards or committees. Reasonable steps have been taken to ensure the accuracy of the information presented. However, the American Diabetes Association cannot ensure the safety or efficacy of any product or service described in this publication. Individuals are advised to consult a physician or other appropriate health care professional before undertaking any diet or exercise program or taking any medication referred to in this publication. Professionals must use and apply their own professional judgment, experience, and training and should not rely solely on the information contained in this publication before prescribing any diet, exercise, or medication. The American Diabetes Association—its officers, directors, employees, volunteers, and members—assumes no responsibility or liability for personal or other injury, loss, or damage that may result from the suggestions or information in this publication.

∞ The paper in this publication meets the requirements of the ANSI Standard Z39.48-1992 (permanence of paper).

ADA titles may be purchased for business or promotional use or for special sales. For information, please write to Lee Romano Sequeira, Special Sales & Promotions, at the address below.

American Diabetes Association
1701 North Beauregard Street
Alexandria, Virginia 22311

Library of Congress Cataloging-in-Publication Data

Loy, Virginia Nasmyth, 1949-
    Real life parenting of kids with diabetes / Virginia Nasmyth Loy.
        p. cm.
    Includes index.
    ISBN 1-58040-083-3 (alk. paper)
      1. Diabetes in children. 2. Diabetes in children—Patients—Home care. I. Title.

RJ420.D5 L697 2001
618.92'462—dc21

2001046106

Contents

Foreword

When I read the manuscript for the first time, I thought how wonderful it would have been if I'd had this book to give to all those families I have worked with for so many years. Let's face it—it's really tough to be a kid or teen and have diabetes. And it's really tough to be a parent of a child with diabetes. This book goes a long way toward easing that burden, touching on so many important issues that help families cope better with the multiple challenges—both physical and emotional—that diabetes presents. If I could pick an overall theme to this book, I believe it would be this: Do everything you can do as a parent, in a loving and supportive way, to provide the structure and organization your child needs to manage diabetes well. It is this balance between love and structure that allows your child the freedom to develop and live his or her life fully with diabetes.

I believe that at its roots, diabetes is about balance—the balance between food and insulin, between high and low blood sugars, and, on a deeper level, between feeling free and feeling limited. Diabetes throws limitations in the faces of children and adolescents at critical developmental stages. Young children seek freedom to play and explore in a safe environment, while adolescents seek independence and a sense of themselves as competent and successful in the world. The struggle against the limits that diabetes imposes can be the source of much difficulty, pain, and family conflict. To manage diabetes well requires a balanced approach. The challenge for you and your child is to meet diabetes head on and not to fall into the traps of denial, avoidance, or outright rebellion against its demands. Virginia shows us that this challenge can be engaged fully by a parent with acceptance, love, courage, and crystal clear communication.

While upbeat in tone, the book does not ignore the difficulties faced by a young person with diabetes. However, by seeing these obstacles as challenges to be managed or opportunities for learning, you are given a way to help your child develop a healthy attitude toward the disease, and move on from there. Diabetes is only a piece of the "pie" that is your child's life; it is not the entire pie. That being said, it is a piece that demands attention. As J.R.R. Tolkien once put it, "It does not do to leave a live dragon out of your calculations, if you live near him." This is not always an easy lesson to learn, but Virginia's book is full of tips, stories, and pieces of advice to help every parent of a child with type 1 diabetes.

The diagnosis of diabetes may leave a child, or family, feeling scared, alone, isolated. You'll find the theme of community as a healing force in this book, over and over again. Support is so important and all too often ignored. Virginia relates story after story of enlisting help, building support networks, and developing relationships with others that serve as resources in time of need. The bonds of family, friends, and community dissolve the isolation into which parents can so easily fall when dealing with diabetes and give you the strength to go on when things seem too tough. The book describes how teens can mentor other young people with diabetes and how to start a diabetes support or play group.

Another strength of the book is its discussion of the emotional roller coaster that diabetes can be for families. Virginia's description of her sons' grieving process and her method of supporting them through that rough period particularly stand out in my mind. Perhaps we should also acknowledge the grieving process of the parent when the image of the perfect, healthy child comes crashing down with the simple dipstick of a urine sample in the doctor's office. The sense of loss, shock, despair, anger, and sadness that families experience at the time of diagnosis and beyond cannot be ignored. We are often left seeking an answer to the question, "Why my child?" As Virginia points out, "life is not fair . . . life is life," and when diabetes hits your family, the only choices you have are what attitude you will take toward it and how you will respond to it. In *Real Life Parenting of Kids with Diabetes*, Virginia shares the personal stories of how her family has struggled through the labyrinth of diabetes with great success. These stories demonstrate time and again the importance of vigilance, responsibility, forethought, organization, and communication. This family has turned its diabetes burden into a blessing—the blessing of a connected, loving family.

We are fortunate to live in an era of great progress in our ability to care for children with diabetes. While science and technology have given us the tools to better control blood sugars and provide for long and healthy lives, the human challenges remain formidable. In the final analysis, *Real Life Parenting of Kids with Diabetes* acknowledges that you have within you everything it takes to give your children the love, support, and guidance they need to become the bright stars on earth they are all destined to be.

With best wishes,
Marc J. Weigensberg, MD

Foreword

Families and friends of juvenile diabetics who are lucky enough to read this book and its companion by Virginia's sons will find them a revelation in their approach to this all-too-common illness. By using a combination of unending energy, optimism, altruism, and knowledge, she has changed the lives of her own family and, indeed, of the entire community in which she lives. She has succeeded in making a team of everyone who comes into contact with her children and other children with juvenile diabetes, which changes the position of the diabetic from odd-man-out to a hero, whose accomplishments are shared by all.

After forty years of dealing with patients with diabetes and other pediatric illnesses, I find this approach revolutionary. Virginia and her family have found amazing success in expanding their accomplishments to change the lives of many other diabetics. I believe that if other parents apply the philosophy and approach described in this book, it will change the lives of the juvenile diabetes community for the better, in a manner and degree never before experienced. I wholeheartedly recommend this book to anyone with an interest in juvenile diabetes.

Martin E. Berger, M.D.

Acknowledgments

I am incredibly proud of how my sons, Spike and Bo, and the rest of our family responded to the challenge of diabetes. This has truly been a journey, a family adventure. My daughters have been generous, helpful, and caring big sisters. Thank you, Jenny and Mary. Thanks to Rick for working hard, for being there, and especially for his enthusiasm for this project. Thanks to my mother, Grandma Virginia, for setting such high standards and for the wonderful relationship she has with my children, and to my extraordinary big sister, Gebo, for her constant support over the years and for all the fun we had editing. Fourteen years ago when Spike and Bo were first diagnosed and they were managing diabetes so well, my sister said, "Virginia, your kids have such great attitudes. When they grow up, they are really going to do something important for kids with diabetes."

So many people in our community helped our family raise Spike and Bo that when they entered high school, the boys felt it was time to give something back. They collaborated on writing a book for kids, *Getting a Grip on Diabetes*. Once the American Diabetes Association had the final draft of *Getting a Grip* in their hands, the boys' editor, Sherrye Landrum, asked me if I would write a companion book for parents. And so the parents' guide was born. Sherrye has been wonderful to work with. She really gets it. She encouraged me to share our personal story. Thank you, Sherrye.

I thank my friends Harriette Erickson, Katharine Wilde, Joan Rush, Mandy MacDonald, and June Behar for carefully going over the first draft of the parents' guide. Their comments and suggestions are deeply appreciated.

When I thought the manuscript was in pretty good shape, I sent it to three wonderful women, people who didn't really know me, moms who have kids with diabetes. Rollie Berry's mother, Susanne, went over the manuscript with a fine-toothed comb. Thank you, Susanne. Julia's mother, Lyra, who I met via e-mail only a week after her daughter was diagnosed, had special insight into what newly diagnosed families need. Laura's mother, Diane Valine, very graciously contributed her knowledge and experience to the toddler section. Thank you, Diane.

Thanks to all the wonderful doctors who reviewed this manuscript and for their contributions. On a personal note, I want to thank Dr. Diana Schwarzbein for her brilliance and hands-on care of my boys. Thanks to Dr. Marc Weigensberg for his enthusiasm and warm support of this project. Dr. Marc is a powerful and positive force, especially for kids with diabetes. We are lucky to know him. Thanks to Dr. Ronald Chochinov, for his work with kids, and for taking the time to review this manuscript with me. A special thanks to Dr. Martin Berger for his wisdom, his compassion, for helping so many, and for taking my sons into his heart.

Speaking of my sons, Spike and Bo, you guys are my heroes.

Introduction

I have two wonderful, successful sons, Spike and Bo, now 19 and 17 years old, who have had diabetes since they were 7 and 6 years old. Spike and Bo thrive, and they do everything! They surf, ski, play all-star soccer, are straight-A students, own cars, date, and are happy kids. Over the years, through trial and error, have figured out how to balance their carbohydrate, exercise, and insulin. They put together a guide for kids, sharing their short cuts and methods, called *Getting a Grip on Diabetes, Quick Tips & Techniques for Kids and Teens*.

When they started giving their book out to kids with diabetes, I began to get phone calls from parents asking what I have learned to help my boys over the past 12 years. This book shares my philosophy for guiding young people through growing up with diabetes. It is meant to be a guide for parents, taken from my years of experience, and a companion book to *Getting a Grip on Diabetes*. I urge you to get the boys' book for your children and family. This book is for you. It, too, is positive and upbeat, but I will address some parent anxieties that your kids don't need to hear about.

Spike and Bodie

My first contact with newly diagnosed families is usually by phone. I try to put families at ease so they can relax, get over being so scared, and get organized. That's what helping kids with diabetes is all about—being organized, informed, and compassionate, and having a sense of humor.

Everything Is Going To Be Okay!

First things first. Keep telling yourself that everything is going to be okay as you begin to set up your child's daily diabetes routine at home and at school. We'll start with 10 quick tips, but there are more sprinkled throughout the chapter.

■ **Everything is going to be all right**
You will learn how to help your child balance carbohydrate, exercise, and insulin. Just be positive as you learn together. Your child's eyesight will be okay, he will grow, he will play sports, he can do well in school.

■ **Where to prick for blood tests**
There is a new meter available, the FreeStyle. With this meter, you prick the top of the forearm. If you are using the finger prick style meter, use the sides of your child's fingertips. Start with the middle and ring fingers.

■ **Where to inject**
Give shots where your child likes it. Mine chose their hips.

■ **How to keep your child safe: The Cooler**
Always have food available. My sons always take a packed cooler to school and on field trips. We always have a packed

cooler in the car. For a list of what to carry in the cooler, see page 22.

∎ **Know your child's symptoms of low and high blood sugars**
Low sugar: headache, empty feeling, shaky hands, upset, crying. **Your child needs sugar.**

High sugar: hyperactive or feels sluggish, breathless, tired, feels bad all over, thirsty.

∎ **Tell everyone your child has diabetes**
Let everyone know your child has diabetes. Give them a list of symptoms for low blood sugar so they can help. (See Symptoms on page 174.)

∎ **Make food easy**
My boys ate every two hours from the age of 6 until they entered high school. Pack snacks for your child in brown bags, write the time he should eat it on the bag, and put the bags in the cooler. Be sure the cooler goes everywhere with him.

∎ **Going to school**
Meet with all your child's teachers. Ask for their help. Give them a list of low blood sugar symptoms (page 174). Give teachers a packed cooler and instructions for how to use it. Visit school often. Help your child get used to blood checks and snacking at school.

∎ **Your child can play all sports**
Exercise will help your child keep his blood sugars level. Hard physical exercise requires more food and less insulin. Give his coaches diabetes information, too.

∎ **Get organized and stay alert**
Get organized so you can make blood checks, shots, and eating part of the daily routine. If you take control of your child's diabetes program, life for the entire family will go more smoothly.

When I contact a new family, either by phone or in person, I begin by giving them some basic information to help them get started handling their child's diabetes. A typical phone call might go like this: "Hi, my name is Virginia Loy. Your name was given to me by one of your friends who asked me to call because I have raised two wonderful little boys with diabetes." (The family is in shock; they usually just listen.) "First, I want you to know that everything is going to be all right. I have been taking care of my boys for 12 years, and they are happy, successful kids. I know you are getting a lot of information right now; I just want you to know you will figure all this out. It can be done. I called because I want to share with you a few things we have learned that might make these first few weeks easier."

YOUR ROUTINE: BLOOD GLUCOSE CHECKS AND SHOTS

Setting up a routine to take care of diabetes helps each day go more smoothly for everyone.

Where to Prick

A more comfortable method of doing blood sugar checks has just become available. Using the FreeStyle or the AtLast meters, you can prick the top of the forearm or the leg. A much smaller drop of blood is used with these meters than with the finger-prick method, and you get a blood sugar reading in 15 seconds. If you use fingers for blood testing, it is more comfortable when you prick on the side of the finger, in the fat along the side of the nail. If you put your fingers down on a tabletop, prick on the part that's not touching the table. The side of the finger isn't as sensitive. Don't worry about which finger your child wants you to prick. My boys like to use their ring fingers and middle fingers. They've been using the same fingers for twelve years, and their fingers are fine.

Lancets

The FreeStyle and AtLast meters come with a lancet device. For finger pricks, there are all kinds of devices out there, but we like the BD Adjustable Lancet Device and ultra fine lancets. The ultra fines are tiny and better to use on kids.

Blood Glucose Meters

I'm sure your doctor has recommended a blood glucose meter. Read the directions. Ask your doctor, nurse, or diabetes educator for help learning how to use it. Meters need to be calibrated. Calibrate your meter on schedule. Keep your equipment in good condition. If you get blood sugar numbers that don't seem right—way too high or way too low for the way your child is acting—double-check your meter's calibration. (Many parents keep two meters handy at all times. That way they can double-check one meter's reading with the second.) If you have an old meter, look into the new models. They work better, faster, and require less blood. Spike and Bo both use the new FreeStyle Meter. Before it came out, Spike used the Lifescan Fasttake. He liked it because of its convenient size, it only takes 15 seconds for a reading, and it uses a very small drop of blood. Bo used the Dex Glucometer. Bo hooks his meter up to his computer and prints out his blood sugars, graphing and charting the numbers. Bo says this really helps him see blood sugar trends. *Diabetes Forecast* magazine puts out a Resource Guide each year that lists all the meters on the market (and all other diabetes equipment and supplies). You might want to read it and discuss your choice with your doctor.

Visual Strips

We use visual Chemstrips at our house as well as meters. BD makes Chemstrips for meters that can also be read by eye. We always have visual strips on hand for backup, to double-check a meter, and in case the battery runs out. There is a psychological thing that goes on with reading blood sugar numbers. Sometimes you'll get a reading like 290 and feel all upset. On the visual strip, it would just look a little darker than 240. That feels okay. A little darker, higher than 240, calls for an extra unit of short-acting insulin. Once in a while, when we're feeling worn out by reading the exact numbers, we'll take a break from our meters and use the visual strips. **Tip: Always take visual Chemstrips on trips in case of a dead battery or lost meter.**

Explaining Arm Pricks or Finger Pricks to Your Child

I have a distinct parenting style, and maybe my approach will work for you. When Spike was first hospitalized with diabetes, the doctors and nurses told us how we would have to do blood tests before every meal, before bedtime, even in the middle of the night (when he was little.) It's a lot to take in for a kid. After we listened and absorbed the information, I looked over to Spike sitting in the hospital bed and began to explain things to him. "Spike," I said, "you have diabetes. You've got a choice. We can do everything the doctor tells us to do, and you'll be well, or you can be sick. Which do you want to do?" Spike said, "I want to be well."

"Good," I said, "me, too. That means we're going to do finger pricks before you eat to see how much sugar is in your blood. That will tell us how much insulin you need. Hey, Spike [a big hug], don't worry. Everything will be all right. Your dad and I are going to take good care of you. I love you. I'm sorry this happened to us, but it did."

Your Emotional Reactions to Blood Checks and Shots

I used to dread doing finger pricks on my little boys' tiny fingers. We have talked about it since they've gotten older, and it definitely bothered me more than it bothered them. Oh, sometimes they hollered and cried, but I found it best to just be matter-of-fact. "Bo," I might say, "I need to do a finger prick. Let's do one right now." When they were little, we made a game of it. We called their middle finger their flip-off finger. They especially liked to hold up their flip-off finger for blood checks. We were always trying to find ways to get free blood for checks. Whenever they fell down and skinned a knee or had a bloody loose tooth, one of their sisters would call out, "Free blood test, get Mom."

The finger pricks bothered me so much that after five years, I went to talk to a family counselor. He helped me see why it was bothering me so much, and maybe hearing about my counseling session will help you. The counselor asked me to close my eyes and talk him through a finger prick. In my description of taking blood from one of my little boy's fingers, I kept referring to their baby hands and their tiny fingers. I saw this giant lancet breaking through their skin. He said, "Virginia, how old are your boys now?" I answered, "11 and 13."

"And how big are their hands?"

"Well," I said, "Bo's are about the size of mine, and Spike's hands are bigger." Bingo! That's all it took. My mind let go of the image of a baby hand. All of a sudden, pricking the finger of a grown-up hand was okay.

Shots

During the first day of diagnosis at the hospital, usually the parents and/or child have already taken over giving the shots. I let

my kids choose where they want to have their shot. My boys' favorite place is on the top of the hip. Imagine you are a farm wife standing with your hands on your hips. That's where we give the shots—right where your hands touch your hip. With athletic kids, we have found the thigh is too hard. When they were little, they liked shots in their arms, especially when shot time was when they were playing baseball, because they didn't have to untuck their shirts.

Syringes

There are different sizes of needles available. The smallest, thinnest needles are called ultra fine. These are best for kids. We use Ultra Fine BD Syringes. Syringes come in different sizes, too. We use $^3/_{10}$ cc syringes. They hold less insulin, so their markings are bigger and easier to read. There are regular length needles and short needles. Many families like the short needles for little kids. My boys used the regular length needles for the first 10 years. At 19, Spike switched to the short needle. It's a matter of what feels better. Sometimes it feels better to inject a little deeper. When your child chooses a needle he likes, stick with it.

Injector

Many people like to hold the syringe and inject right into the skin. My boys like to use an Inject-Ease. This little device has a spring action that rapidly puts the needle into the skin. To use it, Bo fills his syringe with his dose of insulin, drops the syringe into the Inject-Ease, and snaps it in. He holds the Inject-Ease next to his hip, then clicks the button on the Inject-Ease. The needle enters his tissue, then he pushes the plunger down on the syringe, injecting the insulin.

Who Gives the Shots?

Spike went to the hospital on Thanksgiving Day, 1987. We learned as much about diabetes those first days as we could absorb. Bo went to the hospital the following Thanksgiving weekend, in 1988. Once we learned what it took to handle diabetes for a kid, I made the decision to take on the responsibility of managing Spike and Bo's diabetes for as long as they would let me. I decided I would be the best mom of diabetic kids I could be. I had two reasons. Number one, I wanted my boys to have as close to a carefree childhood as possible. Having to face diabetes every two hours, every day, is enough. I told the boys, "I'll work on diabetes, you work on being kids." Second, my husband Rick and I found the responsibility of giving blood tests, figuring the proper amounts of insulin, choosing the right snacks and meals, and preparing a big breakfast every single morning no matter what, to be a very big job.

I wanted the boys to be carefree for as long as possible. It occurred to me that if a very young child has to be responsible for 5 blood tests, 5 shots, 3 meals, and 4 snacks a day, he might be really sick of it by the time he was ready to go away to college. I wanted our boys to take charge of whatever aspects of their diabetes they chose to, but only when they were ready. Then when they went off to college, they would welcome the chance to be in complete control and not be sick of it. You never want a child so overwhelmed by the responsibility of managing diabetes that he rebels and quits taking his insulin.

Spike began giving himself shots around age 12 or 13. Bo chose to do it at the same time as Spike, making it age 11 for him. They still let me give them some of their shots during high school. To this day I ask them if I can draw their insulin once in a while. And when they are sick or hospitalized I take over.

The Logbook

Keeping a log makes life easier. It only takes a minute. When Spike and Bo were young, I wrote down every blood sugar number, insulin dose, snack and meal; we even listed exercise. In the early years when their bodies are changing so rapidly, it is very helpful to have a logbook to look at to figure out what is going on. **Tip: Write down the insulin dose and time of injection *after* you inject. Once in a while, you'll find you can't remember if you've just given an injection or just thought about giving one.**

When Spike and Bo were teens, they began using sophisticated meters that kept their records for them. When everything was running smoothly, they didn't fill in their logbooks every day. The logbook was most useful when their numbers began bouncing around. Their specialist provided an excellent chart for them to track their sugars, carbohydrate, and exercise. At the end of each day, they would connect the dots of their charted blood sugars. This provided a good visual record. (See chart on page 181.)

LEARNING ABOUT FOOD: SHORT, MEDIUM, AND LONG

You will learn to balance carbohydrate, insulin, and exercise. You'll probably go home from the hospital, look into your cupboards, and realize you need to make some changes. It took me some time to figure out food, but this is what we came up with. Bo and Spike were little, and I wanted to make it easy for them, so we began talking about food differently. They liked to call food short, medium, and long.

▪ **Short:** Foods with sugar (carbohydrate) that work fast, such as Gatorade, fruit juice, milk, cookies, and cake frosting.

- **Medium:** Foods that take a little longer to work, such as bread, crackers, cereal, beans, and tortillas (carbohydrate).
- **Long:** Foods that take a long time to get into the system, such as nuts, jerky, cheese, chicken, steak, and hot dogs (protein and fat).

Basically, Spike and Bo knew they needed short foods when their blood sugars were low. For meals and snacks, they would eat a small amount of short food for quick energy, enough medium food for their activity level, and some long foods to make their meals last longer.

Once diabetes came to our family, we all went on the same healthy diet. There were no foods in the house set aside for Dad or other brothers and sisters. No need to hurt the feelings of the kid who has diabetes. We did not keep soft drinks in the house, but if that is your family's habit, you might change to bottled water and diet soft drinks. **Tip: To help your child drink lots of water, buy bottled water by the case—little bottles for the little ones and one-liter sports bottles for teens.**

Having a kitchen stocked with healthy food will make the transition to healthy eating matter-of-fact. I made sure I had certain items in my cupboards, so I could make fast meals and snacks and be prepared for low blood sugars.

For treating low blood sugars, have:

Gatorade	Sugar Popsicles
7-Up	Cereal
Milk	

Checklist for stocking your kitchen

Olive oil	Butter
Whole milk	Cream

Eggs	Bacon
Sausage	Frozen chicken tenders
Frozen steak	Frozen peas
String cheese	Monterey Jack cheese
Cheddar cheese	Whole wheat bread
Whole wheat crackers	Rice
Noodles	Cream of mushroom soup
Potatoes	Green onions

With these basic supplies, you can prepare a balanced breakfast, lunch, or dinner in a hurry. For example: Breakfast burrito, stir-fried chicken with rice, stir-fried beef with rice or potatoes, and beef stroganoff. (See recipes on pages 178.)

Tip: When there is nothing else in the house, you can always cook scrambled eggs.

Tip: My boys never eat carbohydrates alone. We always add a protein (long food) and a little fat. This seems to make food last longer in their systems and helps keep their blood sugars level. This may work the same for you; you'll have to experiment and find out.

Photo by: Shed Behar

Virginia and Grandma Virginia

Get your Neighbors Involved

Once your friends and neighbors know how hard you are working to help your child manage diabetes, they will be there for you. As organized as you might be, there will be days when you need some help. I think my good friend Mandy makes the point in this story:

I will never forget sitting out on my porch one morning, relaxing, having a cup of coffee, when I saw a dust cloud roaring up my driveway. Coming to a screeching halt, out jumps Virginia, hair askew, clad in her old bib overalls. I knew right away that this was an emergency run.

"Mandy, I need something sweet right away, I don't have time to go down the hill to the market," she yelled. We ran into the house, headed for the old kitchen cabinet where I kept a stash of candy and granola bars for such occasions as this (Bodie and Spike's stash). We never made it to the cabinet because Virginia spotted the birthday cake I had made the day before sitting on the counter. She grabbed a big slice of cake and asked if I had any leftover frosting. To my astonishment, she found a container in the refrigerator with just about three tablespoons left in it (With six children, I am lucky if anything is ever left over). Virginia grabbed the cake and frosting. "Thanks Mandy, I'll talk to you later."

In one motion, she was in her car, and the dust cloud was moving back down my driveway and out towards the highway. Later, while I was on the phone with Virginia and she was giving me the "all clear," my son Duncan came downstairs to the kitchen. He was rummaging around the refrigerator, moving containers, combing every corner. . . . Slamming the refrigerator door, Duncan whined, "Hey, who ate the last of the frosting anyway?" I just smiled. **Tip: When you involve your neighbors, they become part of your child's team.**

2

Make the Decision to Take Charge

Here's a little background about making the decision to take charge. When the boys were diagnosed, we read everything we could find on kids and diabetes, and we talked with families who had diabetic kids, successful kids as well as kids struggling to cope. We talked to young adults with diabetes and to our doctors. One theme that kept coming up was, "Watch out for teenage rebellion." Teenagers rebel; that's a given. Teenagers with diabetes may rebel; you just don't want them to rebel against managing their diabetes.

I discovered, mostly through interviewing families, that often the teens who had the roughest time with their diabetes were those who had been in charge of their diabetes for many years. Puberty is a time when daily, even hourly, growth hormones and sex hormones flood the system. Hormones, stress, excitement, and illness interfere with the delivery of insulin. During growth spurts, most teens experience difficult-to-control high blood sugars, which can be frustrating. At this time, they may need expert help to get their blood sugars back under control. Sometimes kids get exhausted trying to balance their body chemistry, and they begin to ignore their blood sugars. To put it simply, they get sick

of the responsibility. The attitude I heard was, "Puberty is a time when blood sugars surge out of control. The teens' bodies are out of control, so why even try?" This attitude can lead to disaster.

Different health professionals had different ideas about who should be in charge, but I saw that the pattern of rebellion emerged most often in adolescents who had to handle all their own care. Tough things happen when you have diabetes—very low blood sugars and very high blood sugars, trips to the hospital, and out-of-control feelings because the blood sugar is too high over a long period of time. This is why the adults in our family chose to be in charge of our boys' diabetes regimen for as long as possible. It appears to be working for us. The boys work hard to check their blood sugars and take the appropriate amounts of insulin 4 or 5 times a day. At 17 and 19, they haven't been doing it for so long that they are fed up with the responsibility. Whenever they are sick, I volunteer to set up their blood test or draw their insulin to give them some rest.

Getting Organized to Make your Child Safe

You can do this! It's a lot to learn, but getting organized will help keep your child safe when he is away from home. Any child with diabetes already has a lot on his mind. Every school day, to help things run smoothly, I checked on our supplies. This way, when Bo walked out the door to catch the school bus, I knew his kit was packed, his lunch was in his cooler, and he could concentrate on being a kid.

If you take charge of the nuts and bolts of diabetes, your child will benefit. He or she will know you really care, and your child will feel safe. A great deal of anxiety will be avoided, and the world won't seem so scary. Kids want to feel well, and they try hard, but they are kids. It takes an organized adult mind to be on top of exercise, insulin, and food—and to do this every day. Besides, sometimes things don't go well—so you'll need to be a calm problem-solver. For instance, let's say you figure the insulin dose one morning, and then your daughter does not eat her toast, picks at her bacon, and goes off to school. Two hours later, she has a pretty bad low at school, so the teacher gives her a drink of Gatorade and a granola bar and calls you. You drive over to the school to reassure your daughter that everything is going to be all right. The two of you talk about what happened.

The conversation might go like this. "Let's see, I gave you 8 units of R (short-acting insulin) this morning and 8 units of NPH (intermediate-acting insulin that starts working in two hours). You weren't really hungry this morning and didn't eat any toast. Hmm. Looks like I gave you a little too much insulin for the breakfast you had. Tell you what. Tomorrow morning I'll give you a little less insulin if you're not hungry. We can talk about what you feel like eating before we give you your shot. If I had paid attention and realized you didn't eat your toast, we could have packed some crackers for you to eat at 9 AM."

Sounds relatively simple, yes? Now look at the alternative. Your child figures out her insulin dose morning after morning by herself. She has several bad lows at school. She is a young girl, so she doesn't completely understand how to balance carbohydrate, insulin, and exercise. Maybe she was nervous because she had to read aloud in class that morning and now here she is shaky, clammy, and low. After a while, if your child has total responsibility for her insulin and her body is out of control, the poor kid may think to herself, "I'm doing everything right, taking my insulin, eating, and still I feel bad. I get low all the time. I can't handle this."

We don't want our kids to think they can't do this. We can help them learn how, but it takes a lot of years to really get a handle on managing diabetes. There will be many times when the insulin and carbohydrate don't match. I'd rather have my kid depend on me to figure it out after a series of lows. After all, I told my child I would take care of him.

This Is Why Every Morning Mom or Dad should:

▮ Pack the Kit
▮ Pack the Coolers
▮ Put snacks and lunches in brown bags on top
▮ Make sure emergency supplies are at school in the teacher's desk and in the car
▮ Make sure everyone dealing with your child has a copy of Symptoms (page 174)
▮ Make sure everyone dealing with your child knows what to do when your child is low
▮ Remind your child to check in with you if he or she doesn't come home right after school

The following descriptions of the Kit and the Cooler are taken from my boys' book. The Kit goes everywhere your child goes and contains:

▮ Insulin bottles
▮ Syringes (plenty extra just in case) or insulin pen
▮ An injecting device if you use one
▮ Lancets
▮ A finger pricker
▮ Alcohol swabs (optional, Spike and Bo don't use them)
▮ A glucose monitor and strips
▮ Test strips that can be read by eye
▮ Frosting or glucose gel (in case you get really low)
▮ A granola bar
▮ Identification saying who you are, that you have diabetes, and lists emergency contacts, and perhaps, basic procedures for what to do if you are found unconscious
▮ A small notebook

The little Cooler goes with your child **to school and everywhere else**. It contains:

▌ Low blood sugar foods, such as
  • Gatorade
  • Granola bar
  • Frosting
  • Crackers (Cheez-Its), and jerky or peanuts to eat after a low
▌ Snacks in brown bags labeled with the time to eat them

To keep things organized at home, we've set up a Diabetes Drawer in the kitchen. It is where the boys draw up their insulin. It contains extras of the same things that are in their insulin Kits when not in use, minus the ice pack and the insulin, which go in the refrigerator.

THE ONE-YEAR ANNIVERSARY: WHEN IT ALL SINKS IN FOR YOUR CHILD

This may be tough to read. But if you know it's coming, maybe it won't be so hard. Kids seem to do real well adjusting to all that goes with having diabetes. I was amazed at how Spike, diagnosed in the first grade, never complained, was nice about having blood tests and shots, cooperated about eating even when he really didn't want to, etc. Bo was so relaxed about having diabetes that we couldn't believe it. In his words, he had seen his older brother get blood tests and shots and eat all the time, and he thought that's just what kids did. He cried a lot at shot time but he, too, never complained. Then came the one-year anniversary. I have had many phone calls from parents who relate similar stories to me. At first, their kids accept diabetes. Then about a year after they are diagnosed, some serious emotional reactions set in.

This is the hardest thing we experienced in the first years. It was the same with both boys, and you can expect it to happen in your family, too. Around the one-year anniversary, my older son started crying one afternoon. (When little kids get

diabetes, they don't quite realize that it is forever. After a year, the reality of it hits.) He was really crying, out of control crying, sobbing. I held him, and I knew what was wrong. Spike was going through the grieving process. Kids with diabetes mourn the loss of their childhood, just like you would mourn the loss of a loved one. I thought my heart would break when this happened to Spike. Here's what helped: I held Spike in my arms. (The next year it was Bo in my arms.) I helped Spike give words to what he was feeling, but I made it simple. I said, "I love you, Spike, and I will always be here to take care of you." He cried some more. I said, "It's not fair that we got diabetes. It's not fair that it happened to you." Everybody cried. "But it happened, and your dad and I are going to take good care of you."

I had a big, long cry with my son. It seemed like it lasted for hours. I patted him, and held him and repeated over and over again, "Spike, I promise you, everything will be all right."

This emotional reaction, Spike's grieving, was over that day. There were other emotional times, but none as wrenching as the first. With Bo it happened the same way, only this time I expected it. I cried right along with Bo, held him, agreed with him that it wasn't fair and, most importantly, assured him over and over that everything was going to be all right. When the kid stopped crying, I stopped crying, and we went on.

If you find that your child is deeply upset about his diabetes, realize that children experience the grieving process, too. Make sure that you tell your child you are there, and you will take care of him or her.

Finally, if blood sugars are out of control, call your specialist. If emotions seem out of control, if you or your child just can't get it together, or if your child tells you he is really scared and can't handle it, seek professional help.

CONSTANT VIGILANCE

Diabetes is a manageable condition. Your goal each day will be to help your child feel well. Kids want to feel good, do well in school, and play hard. Your child will do his part, but as you are finding out, understanding how to balance carbohydrate, insulin, and exercise is a big responsibility. I think it is much too big a responsibility to give a young child. When I signed up to be a mother, I wanted to be the best mother I could possibly be. When my boys got diabetes, I simply had to add managing diabetes to the list of what I do for my kids.

Follow a Schedule

The following is Spike and Bo's schedule. We lived by this schedule when the boys were little. I urge you to share your child's schedule with friends, coaches, and teachers. When adults see this schedule, it helps them understand your child and diabetes. Then they can help. (Adjust the times on this schedule to fit your child's routine. Follow your doctor's advice. Sometimes rapid-acting insulin and NPH are taken at the same time; sometimes the doses are staggered.)

Schedule

8:00 AM	Blood sugar check
	Insulin injection R (or rapid-acting) and NPH
	Breakfast
10:00 AM	Snack - NPH kicks in (longer-lasting insulin)
12:00 PM	Blood sugar check
	Insulin injection R (or rapid-acting insulin)
	Lunch
2:00 PM	Snack
	Blood sugar check

4:00 PM	Snack
6:00 PM	Blood sugar check
	Insulin injection R (or rapid-acting insulin)
	Dinner
8:00 PM	Blood sugar check
	Insulin injection NPH (long-lasting insulin)
2:00 AM	(When they were very young) Blood sugar check

We work hard every day to balance our child's chemicals and keep his blood sugar normal. Many things influence how insulin is absorbed and how blood sugar levels go up and down. You need to know what they are. This list comes from our own experiences. Your child will probably have different experiences, but this list can help you be aware and prepared.

Things That Lower Blood Sugar

▌ **Exercise:** Lowers blood sugar rapidly. During soccer games, basketball, football, swim meets, etc., your child may need to snack every 15 minutes, and do a blood test at halftime.

▌ **Stress:** During exams and times of heavy concentration, the brain absorbs enormous amounts of sugar. Blood sugar can drop dramatically, causing lapses in mental function. When sugars are low, your child just can't think. A snack and a 5–10 minute break to absorb the carbohydrate will get her back on track.

▌ **Cold weather or cold water:** Lowers blood sugar rapidly.

▌ **Hot weather:** Changes insulin needs.

▌ Too much insulin, not enough carboyhdrate.

Special Events That Lower Blood Sugar

▌ Birthday parties

▌ Christmas morning

▌ Christmas Eve, in anticipation of Christmas morning

- Halloween (page 149) and Easter morning
- The night before vacations, field trips, fishing trips, a visit to Grandma's
- Acting in a school play or playing an instrument in front of an audience
- Spelling bees
- Chess tournaments or any competition that takes lots of concentration

Things That Can Raise Blood Sugar

- **Growth spurts and hormones:** Usually cause a rise in blood sugar, which can make your child feel hyper. Very high blood sugar usually causes tiredness, sluggishness, and that all-over sick feeling.
- **Stress:** Exams, excitement, anticipation, being in trouble at home or at school.
- **Too little insulin:** You figured the insulin dose wrong.
- **Too much food:** Sometimes your child is hungry and eats more than he planned.
- **Sugar drinks, snacks, cookies, cake, and candy:** These will do it every time, which is why they are eaten when kids' sugars are low.
- **Illness:** Usually causes a rise in blood sugar but may cause a low. When your child is ill, she may take 2 or 3 additional shots of R or rapid-acting insulin per day to control blood sugar. You need to do frequent blood sugar checks and check for ketones, too (page 115).

Learning to Check Every Two Hours

As an adult, you realize that, until a cure is found, your child will be handling diabetes every two hours, every day. Once you accept this, your task gets easier. Why every two hours? Young children are very active and use up a lot of calories. We found that by giving our kids a snack every two hours, they were able to keep their sugars above 80 mg/dl. That means you will need to be aware of what your child is doing every two hours. Does he need a snack? Did he eat it? Sometimes when kids are busy playing with their friends, they forget to snack, and they crash. (My kids call having a low blood sugar level—under 60—crashing.) Crashing is no fun. Depending on how severe the low is, it can be scary for your child. So it's better to help them remember to graze. We found that once you establish a routine, like the one you have on school days, lows happen less often. But when you break the routine, like on the weekend or during vacations, crashes happen more frequently. I often wonder why we don't learn, but sometimes we just forget to snack on schedule.

If your child is taking 3 shots a day, you will be doing blood checks before breakfast, before lunch, and before dinner. Depending on how your child's blood sugars are, you may be doing before-bed blood checks, even at 2 AM. Nobody likes blood checks, but when my kids were little, I used to say, "Thank God for blood tests. They are a great tool for keeping your sugars normal."

A final note about constant vigilance. **The sooner you make up your mind to always be vigilant, the happier your family life will be.** It feels good to do a good job.

ALWAYS HELP WHEN YOUR CHILD IS LOW

Classic symptoms of low blood sugar are: headache; stomachache; feeling empty; shaky hands; feeling faint; and being very upset, angry, or crying. It is not always obvious. Sometimes your child may be out of sorts or feel grouchy or sluggish, or is studying and just can't figure out a simple math problem. When I see one of my kids acting a little off, or if he really looks pale or shaky or clammy, I say, "Hey, Bo, need some?" That alerts him. But, if the child is very low, he may not be thinking well enough to get up, go to the cupboard, and get his snack. Typically if I notice a very low child, I talk to him while I'm getting a glass of **milk**. We have delicious chocolate chip cookies, graham crackers, and small trick-or-treat sized candy bars in the house for lows. **First we treat the low. Then we check his blood sugar.** If the kid is low, we have already started treating the low. If he is very high, and we were wrong, no harm done. We have the option of injecting 2 or 3 units of Regular or Humalog.

Candy bars aren't the best choice if their blood sugar is dropping quickly, because the fat in the candy bar slows down the absorption of the carbohydrate in it. That's the time for milk or juice. For severe lows, when they can't drink, we use frosting or glucose gel, or glucagon if they're really out of it.

Mood Swings

Generally kids are pretty happy people. You may notice, though, that when your child is experiencing pretty high blood sugar (240 plus) he feels grouchy, and tired, or he just can't do simple tasks—no matter how hard he tries. You may notice this with his homework; he gets frustrated with his work or keeps trying to do the same problem over and over. I can honestly say that the few times I have gotten after one of my boys for being in a bad mood, I regretted it. Before you criticize your kid for being grumpy, look at his blood sugar. Sure, kids have moods, but it is almost always high blood sugar that alters their normally rosy dispositions. Consider this. If the kid is high, he feels awful. He can feel sore all over like he has the flu. You can help take care of this by noticing the mood, helping with a blood check (if he is really feeling awful, he won't want to do it), and then figuring out how much extra insulin to give.

I don't generally point out to my boys that I suspected they were high because they were acting stubborn or out-of-sorts. I keep that information to myself and help them. In a few minutes, the episode is behind us. To build a kid who feels confident and positive about himself requires matter-of-fact dealing with the little negative things diabetes throws at them. I don't think chipping away at their character by reminding them of how ornery they were serves any purpose.

When Your Child Doesn't Feel Right, Check His Sugar

In our house when a kid feels bad, has a headache, feels sick, is grumpy, giddy—you name it—we check his sugar. It can be kind of funny sometimes. Recently Bo complained of a headache. I said, "Let's check your sugar." We checked his sugar just to be sure. Because his head hurt so much, he checked for ketones. (See page 115.) His sugar wasn't particularly high, and there were no ketones, which indicated that his sugar hadn't been running high for many hours. After checking everything, I was able to say, "Bo, guess what, you've got a headache."

"I told you so," he said.

"Yes, but now we know." He took two Tylenol. End of headache.

3

Toddlers

I turned to our friends Jeff and Diane Valine, for advice on handling toddlers with diabetes. Their beautiful three-year-old daughter Laura was diagnosed at age two. Laura is in our playgroup, Kids With Diabetes, so we have gotten to know this precious little girl and her folks. Here is Diane's story (with some comments from me, too):

These are some of the issues that are special to dealing with a little one. I don't know if our experiences are common to all toddlers, but I suspect most of them are. My best advice is to do the best that you can each day, and when you make a mistake, try to forgive yourself promptly.

We try to let Laura lead as normal a three-year-old life as possible, but I admit the idea of sending her to preschool scares me to death. I know it must have been very difficult for Virginia to trust others to care for her boys as they were growing up.

Low Blood Sugar Indicators

The best indicator of how Laura's blood sugar is doing is her behavior. I cannot always tell if she is high or low, but I typically know when she is not feeling well because she is too quiet or irritable. At that point, I usually do a blood check, even if it is not the normal time (before breakfast, lunch, and dinner and at bedtime).

Tantrums

During a tantrum, we always test to rule out high or low blood sugar. If she is within the normal range, we ignore her or she takes a timeout.

I know that sometimes she feels upset because of the diabetes and wants to have some control. We try to give her lots of cuddles and comfort when she's feeling that way because she's right, it isn't fair!

Refusal to Eat

Laura often doesn't want to eat on schedule or eat what she is supposed to. When this happens, we try to get her started on something she really likes—a few Cheerios or a Graham cracker usually works. Once she gets started eating, she usually eats pretty well. I often explain to her that the food and insulin will make her feel better.

Play Dates and Other Fun Activities

Reduce insulin and watch closely. When emotions run high, Laura tends to get low. We watch for clumsy actions or unusual behavior. Laura is a very independent and stubborn little girl. When she starts telling us "I can't do it," it's an indicator that something is wrong. We always carry juice, raisins, candy, and tubes of cake icing. When Laura is acting defiant, we offer the juice or candy first. We explain that if she doesn't eat or drink, she will have to have frosting. If she refuses to eat, we proceed quickly to the frosting. (We squirt frosting between her cheek and gums where it can be absorbed without causing choking.)

Special events may lower blood sugar. At Laura's two-year birthday party, just after she was diagnosed, we made a sugar-free cake. (In the beginning, we were carefully monitoring everything she ate.) After all the excitement of the party, and eating the very sensible sugar-free cake, Laura had a severe low (low blood sugar). For Laura's three-year birthday party, we bought a regular cake and sugar-free ice cream. She was very excited at her birthday party and ran around with the kids for awhile. At the time of her normal afternoon snack, I checked her blood sugar—and it was 62. I decided it was time for cake and ice cream.

We have decided that for some of life's special events, we need to relax and let her experience them just like everybody else. That means cake and ice cream at birthday parties. We can check her blood sugar and adjust her insulin if needed.

Choosing Your Battles

On decisions that are nonnegotiable, like when to eat, we stand our ground. If we can let Laura make some decisions for herself, like what clothes to wear, we do. She loves to wear pretty clothes, that is, fancy dresses even when she's playing in the dirt. It makes Laura feel good and, in the big scheme of things, it doesn't really matter if she gets her clothes dirty. I try not to get upset if she wants something other than traditional breakfast foods for breakfast. A sandwich is okay if she will eat it.

The Toddler Breakfast

A typical breakfast for a toddler should include protein and carbohydrates. But toddlers don't always eat balanced meals. With toddlers who are picky eaters, play it safe. **See what they eat first, then inject the regular or rapid-acting insulin.**

Some mornings we can only coax Laura to eat a few ounces of Rice Chex or Cheerios with a few Fruit Loops sprinkled on top, or a waffle with sugar-free syrup, or toast with butter. Breakfast is our most challenging meal because Laura is sort of a sleepyhead and isn't usually too anxious to eat. Some of her non-traditional meals might be a peanut butter and sugar-free jelly sandwich or pizza. At times, the only thing I can get her to eat is a cookie. This has been a tough one for us, and we still struggle with it.

Toddler Breakfast Ideas

If your toddler is picky, try adding different proteins along with the carbs at breakfast until you find something he will eat. My boys love scrambled eggs and would be happy to eat scrambled eggs every single day. Try:

- A bowl of cereal with whole milk, and bacon, cheese, or sausage. (The whole milk contains fat and lasts longer.)
- A scrambled egg. Scramble eggs in butter with a tablespoon of heavy whipping cream per egg. Cream makes the eggs sweeter and adds fat, which lasts longer.
- Bacon, ham, sausage, or tiny pieces of stir-fried steak.
- Half a potato, diced and fried in butter with melted jack cheese.
- Whole wheat toast with peanut butter, cream cheese, or melted cheese.

Whether or not your child eats all of his breakfast won't matter if you adjust and inject the rapid-acting insulin after breakfast. I found that the boys liked "ranch" breakfasts: bacon, eggs, and fried potatoes with melted cheese. After eating two or three proteins and a carb, they had better blood sugars throughout the morning hours. You'll have to experiment a bit with your child. When you find something your toddler will eat, stick with it. My boys have had approximately the same breakfast, just increasingly larger servings, for 10 years, and they still like it!

Typical Toddler's Schedule

Diane thought it would be helpful for parents to see Laura's schedule. The amount of insulin that toddlers take is very small considering their weight and eating habits. Laura is 3 years old and weighs 35 pounds.

Laura's Schedule:

7:00 AM	Wake up and check blood sugar
7:15–7:30	Eat breakfast
7:35	Insulin - 1 unit Humalog, 4.5 units N. The amount of Humalog is dependent on her morning blood sugar reading. If it is below 75 mg/dl, I usually give her a half unit.
9:30	Blood check and snack
12:00 PM	Blood check and lunch
12:30–2:00	Nap
2:00–2:30	Blood check and snack
5:00	Blood check and dinner
7:30	Blood check and snack

We don't check Laura's blood sugar in the middle of the night. I know many others do, but our endocrinologist doesn't think it is necessary for her. However, if Laura wakes in the night, we do check. (For the first couple of years, we often had to test Bo at 2 AM. He had many lows in the middle of the night. He has always been more sensitive to insulin than Spike.)

Delaying Bedtime

Laura has figured out that she can delay bedtime by eating her snack slowly. This is a problem we are currently working with, and I don't really have a solution other than to start early and to threaten to put her to bed anyway. Sometimes we tell her no bedtime stories if she doesn't eat (which is about the worst punishment for her), and she'll usually start eating.

Potty Training

We have found that when Laura has high blood sugars, she may have accidents and not make it to the bathroom in time. When she has an accident, we suspect high blood sugar and check it.

Remaining Flexible

We try to stay flexible and look carefully at Laura's readings (blood sugar numbers) before giving her morning insulin dose. If she wakes up with 48 mg/dl, we don't give her the same amount of Humalog we would if it were 200. We often give Humalog insulin in $1/_2$-unit increments because Laura is very sensitive to it. We do this by trying to find the mid-point between the two lines on the syringe.

Support

If you are new to diabetes, try to find someone to support you who has been through it. A mother of a child with diabetes was at our door the day after Laura was diagnosed and helped us tremendously.

Babysitters

Babysitters are another tough issue. I feel very fortunate to have a close neighbor who takes care of my children. She is a wonderful mom with a great deal of common sense. She contacts me during the day when she has a problem or is looking for recommendations on what to do. I have e-mail at work, I carry a cellular phone, and my husband, Jeff, carries a pager. We don't limit how many blood checks she does a day. If there's a question in her mind, we have told her to check, but Laura's behavior is very indicative of how she's feeling. When she is happy and outgoing and funny, she's usually in the correct range. If she's grouchy, a couch potato, or quiet and cuddly, then she's probably high or low.

Preschool

Laura wanted to go to school. We wanted her to have as normal a childhood as possible, so we began looking for a healthy environment where she could safely have fun and socialize with other kids her age. I called the preschool my older son had attended. I knew it was a loving, nurturing environment. Laura and I toured the facility. There was a big play area, artwork drying on the bathroom floor, and Laura found that they had kid-sized potties. She was impressed. I talked to the preschool director about Laura's diabetes and asked if they would consider accepting her in the program. Laura was invited to attend. A week before school started, we did a training with the teachers. The director attended, as did Laura's new teacher, the teacher's assistant, the teacher in the classroom next door, and the Early Birds teacher. At the end of the training, a few of the teachers were looking a little pale, and I could tell they were uneasy about what they had agreed to do.

The first day of school, I stayed in a workroom adjacent to Laura's classroom and was glad I did. I was able to encourage the teachers and help them get comfortable using her meter. The teachers discovered that Laura has a tendency to get low at recess. (Now we reduce her insulin each school day.) Her teachers asked if they could check Laura's blood sugar before and after recess. Laura often gets a special snack before recess if her blood sugar isn't over 200. Her teacher either calls or sends me a note to let me know how Laura did each day.

Last Friday was Laura's Christmas program at school, and she was magnificent! Her teacher told me she had trouble singing without smiling. She knew all of the finger plays and most of the words to the songs. Laura's teacher thanked me for trusting them to learn to care for her special needs because she was such a fun person to have in class. Wow, how did we get so lucky!

Very Low Blood Sugar Episode

This was an extremely traumatic event for us the first time it happened. For some reason, we were really worried we were going to give her too much frosting, and so the low lasted longer than it needed to. Laura had a serious low at her babysitter's last July. Her blood sugar was 29. The babysitter gave her frosting, but she started to convulse. When the sitter tested her blood sugar, it was in the 80s. (We later found out that the convulsions probably raised her blood sugar.) They put her in the car and took her to the emergency room. When I arrived soon after, I could hear Laura crying. I went back to where she was and stood near her as they drew blood, etc. I rubbed her blankie on her cheek to try to help soothe her. There was a heart monitor and an automatic blood pressure cuff attached to her. She was very upset. The nurse asked if she liked any songs, and we sang "The Itsy Bitsy Spider" to her. She began to calm down. The pulse monitor cuff was on her finger, and Laura is a thumb sucker. It was really bothering her. I asked if they could move it to the other hand, and they said that since she was calm they would take it off. They found us a rocking chair, and we rocked and cuddled for a while. The blood check showed that she was indeed hypoglycemic. We stayed at the emergency room for several hours.

Before she was released, I had to insist that they feed her. I was very concerned that some time had passed, and she had not eaten. You may find that you know more about your child and diabetes than some of the hospital staff. When we went to see her endocrinologist later, he asked if the babysitter had given her an injection of glucagon. We said, "No, she didn't have any." He immediately wrote a prescription with 8 refills. Make sure your babysitter has one and knows how to use it.

Laura gets low from time to time. The first low was memorable because we were naive and weren't sure how much sugar to give. The next low was very different. Her symptoms changed. We were accustomed to her being irritable when she had high blood sugar, but with this low, Laura became furious, crying inconsolably, hitting, and kicking. We tried to give her real Coke, but she was unwilling to eat or drink. Then we gave her frosting, which eventually worked.

Tip: You can use glucose gel to treat low blood sugars. Practically speaking, many parents use tubes of cake decorating frosting because they are cheaper, so you tend to keep more tubes around the house—and it works.

Glucagon Injections

Parents, babysitters, and caregivers should read the directions on the glucagon box and know how to use it before they need it. Basically, you would use ½ a dose for a toddler. Glucagon is a hormone that interrupts the action of insulin and raises blood glucose. See page 107.

Parental Fear and Anger

This is embarrassing to tell, but it may be helpful to others. Sometimes when Laura gets low, Jeff and I fall into a trap of yelling at each other out of frustration. As time progresses, we are learning to focus on treating the low, and we try to treat each other respectfully. It is very stressful during lows. If one dose of frosting hasn't brought her around after a minute or two, we treat again and repeat until she comes around. We usually offer her sweets between squirts of frosting because if she eats, it shows that she's coming around. Then we give her a more substantial snack of crackers and cheese or half a sandwich. She is usually hungry after a low.

Laura has had a few lows when we were on the road traveling, usually to somewhere exciting. As we left our house Christmas morning to go to Grandma's, Laura got low. Again, I think that it's the excitement factor.

Excitement Can Cause Low Blood Sugar

Diane's views of handling diabetes with a toddler reminded me of a few things that happened when the boys were young. We were up early to get ready to go to Catalina, a very exciting time for a 6-year-old boy. Bo couldn't function and started having convulsions. I grabbed a tube of frosting and put all of it between his cheeks and gums. Within three minutes, he began responding, and in five, he could drink. (When a child is convulsing, he is more likely to choke or aspirate what you are giving him to drink, so this is the time to use a glucagon injection. That was our next option if he didn't respond to the frosting.) It took twenty minutes to get him back into good shape, but he was absolutely fine, and we left for Catalina that morning as planned. He recovered and had a wonderful trip. I was a wreck for two weeks. Boy, when little kids get excited, they sure crash.

Photo by: Scott Loy

Glucagon

Glucagon works because it is a hormone that instantly interrupts the delivery of insulin. When you inject glucagon in the leg, butt, arm, or anywhere, the insulin in a child's system quits working. (With a toddler, it would be ½ a dose.) The body, especially the liver, dumps sugar into the bloodstream and that is why the child comes around. It is the recommended treatment for an unconscious or convulsing child with low blood sugar.

Once your child is conscious and able to swallow, follow with anything he will and can eat. Finally, wrap up the episode with a substantial meal (with carbs and protein) to sustain him for several hours.

About half the time, kids throw up after a glucagon injection. That's okay. Don't panic. The glucagon has stopped the insulin from working, and their blood sugar should still come up. Be sure to keep your child lying on his side, so if he vomits, he won't aspirate it or choke.

Tight Control

As the Valines did with Laura, we controlled the heck out of Spike that first year—no cake at school parties, etc. But like Diane and Jeff, we found that if kids are exercising and excited, often their sugars don't get too high. Then, after a year of trying so hard to do everything perfectly with Spike, all of a sudden we had two kids to monitor. When we lightened up and didn't worry so much about a little high sugar, we had more fun—and fewer lows. The lows still happened though, at the rate of about one pretty bad low every two weeks per boy, which amounted to somebody having a serious low, head down on desk or sitting down on the playground, about once a week. When this happened, their friends or teachers would grab candy, Gatorade, or juice out of their coolers and give it to the boys.

Diane is right—you need someone who is also living with a child with diabetes to help you. People need to get matched up for support.

The Preschool Option

There is a wide range of opinions on this subject. We didn't send our kids to preschool because I liked having them at home.

I don't think parents should feel they are depriving their toddlers of a learning experience if preschool doesn't work out. Laura was already a nicely socialized little girl, but she wanted to go to school. You need to do what works for your family. There are some problems with preschool for kids with diabetes, for instance, exposure to many childhood colds and flu. At our house, things get tough when the boys are sick. We avoid the flu if at all possible, including getting a flu shot every year!

Attitude About Going to the Hospital

Many times over the years I have said, "Thank God for the hospital." When things get out of hand at home, we can go to the hospital, get put on IVs for fluid, and get back into balance. Both my boys have very good attitudes about going to the hospital for help. I wanted them to look at the emergency room as a comforting place, not a scary place to go. This takes a very positive attitude on the part of the parents. It may be hard, but it's necessary.

In the Hospital, Work with your Medical Team

We have had at least three experiences in a hospital setting where the staff didn't know anything about managing diabetes. I do the insulin shots, and I draw the insulin. If a nurse insists that she do it, then I check on what she has drawn, and we discuss the dose. I must agree, or it doesn't happen. This is important. You are the expert on your child.

Doctors and nurses who don't deal with diabetes on a daily basis can't be expected to know how small an amount of insulin very young, active children need. Some kids are simply more sensitive to insulin. For example Bo, a high-energy kid, and

Laura, because of her weight, both respond immediately to insulin. Spike, on the other hand, has always reacted more slowly to insulin. Children new to insulin therapy or kids in tight control may react more quickly to insulin.

Eating After a Low

We have had a few lows where Spike or Bo kept eating for half an hour. We didn't care how high they got, just as long as they stayed awake and got over that sinking feeling. We don't usually give any scheduled insulin for an hour or so after a super low. We let the kid get back to feeling like himself. Then we would consider how much long-lasting insulin was still in his system, if any—for instance, NPH, which kicks in 2 hours after injecting and works hardest 6–10 hours later. Finally, we check his blood and then inject only a small amount of rapid-acting insulin if needed.

The Embarrassing Stuff

Don't kid yourself; everybody finds it stressful when their children suffer very low blood sugar episodes. Recently a mom shared this story with me. Before leaving for work one morning, she left careful instructions for her husband about breakfast and the amount of Humalog to give their newly diagnosed little boy. Her husband didn't give their son any insulin that morning and sent him off to school. The boy's blood sugar went to 500. A lot of yelling went on in that household that night, and the mom was very angry. She was disappointed that her husband would not take charge. My advice to her was to get over it, and try exploring some alternatives. Perhaps the father did not know enough to help her or have enough experience to overcome his fears and gain confidence that he could do it. Until he could come up to speed, she would have to be in charge.

If both parents trust each other to do insulin, food, and exercise right, then once in a while, each could take a day off from being in charge. On the other hand, if one of you isn't so good at something, say figuring out the food, then the other should do that part of the routine.

Help Each Other

If parents find themselves hollering at each other during the stressful low times, they should realize that all that anxiety and fear has to come out some way. It's better that the yelling is between the adults, allowing the kids to be out of the fear/ anger loop.

If you should find yourselves in this situation, here is something that may help. Sometime when you are both up and feeling friendly, try talking about how each of you could express your fear without hurting the other. Honestly, it helps to rehearse lines that say the words you need to hear. For instance, you say, "I can't believe how terrible and scared I'm feeling right now because our baby's blood sugar is 49." And the other person says, "Me, too. But, don't worry honey, **everything will be all right.** I'm here to take care of you and our son." You can take turns so one of you can be the weak one and the other can say the positive scripted stuff. It works.

COLLECTED TIPS

Write down the insulin dose and time of injection *after* you inject. Once in a while you just can't remember if you've just given an injection or just thought about giving one.

Never eat carbohydrate alone. Always add a protein (long food) and a little fat. This makes food last longer in the system and helps keep blood sugars level.

Keep a packed Cooler by the front door, in the car and at school. (You pack it.) Tape a copy of "Symptoms" inside the top of each cooler.

Always help when your child is low.

When your child is out of sorts—check his sugar.

Mom and Dad: to get your child to exercise, exercise with him.

We have found that following strenuous exercise, warm muscles absorb sugar for four to eight hours. After a hard day of exercising, the nighttime dose of short-acting insulin is usually lowered. You might lower the dose by half or even take only a quarter dose. In some cases, they may take no short-acting insulin at night.

Always give your child a bedtime snack.

Always follow insulin with a small snack, even when they are high. Kids are more comfortable when their sugars come down gradually.

If you give your kid's friends enough information, and allow them to help, they will become your child's best allies.

4

Elementary School

Spike and Bo were fortunate to attend a small rural school where everybody knew everybody else. It was a big deal when Spike, in the first grade, came down with diabetes. All the teachers, kids, and the principal wanted to help. So we figured out ways for the community to help us. This is important. **You will need community support so your child can prosper and be safe.** Here's how we set things up for our boys.

Meet With Teachers (Every Single One)

I have had a meeting with every teacher and every principal at every school they attended, elementary school, junior high, and high school. The first time I went to the school and met with the principal and Spike's teacher, I didn't really know that much about diabetes, but I knew I needed help, so I asked for their help. We put together a list of low blood sugar symptoms for each teacher and even the school secretary. (See Symptoms on page 174.)

Procedure for Meeting with Teachers

Sometime during summer vacation, make an appointment to meet with every teacher the week before school starts. I also met with the principal. Grade school meetings went like this. I showed up at the meeting with a copy of "Symptoms for low blood sugars," their insulin and eating schedule, and something the kids and I had written called "What Everybody Needs to Know so They Can Help." (See page 177.) I gave each teacher, secretary, and the principal a copy of each of the printouts. We would all be sitting around a conference table, and I would begin. I told them that we were trying as hard as we could to keep Spike and Bo's blood sugars normal. I told them it was very hard to keep them level and that I needed their help. Then I asked the teachers what I could do to help my boys in school. What could I do to help the teachers work with my boys, and did they have any advice? This approach empowers others. They become a part of the "team" who are watching over your kids.

I found that asking for help from the professionals was the best possible approach. They jumped at the chance to help my boys. We discussed low blood sugar symptoms, read over my printouts, and then I handed each of them an emergency kit for their desk drawers. This was simply a reclosable plastic bag containing a tube of frosting, a granola bar, and a 6 oz. can of apple juice.

I explained how to use the emergency kit and warned them that:

■ **Low blood sugars can happen fast:** It's amazing how quickly low blood sugars can occur and how fortunate we were when Spike or Bo noticed when they were low.
■ **They need to eat:** The boys needed to eat the minute they felt low.

■ **Low blood sugars can sneak up:** If Bo acted funny, listless, stared off, or put his head down on the desk, the teacher should walk up to him and help him drink some juice or Gatorade. Once he's more alert, the teacher should open a granola bar and make sure he ate it. You have to explain to people that when kids are suffering very low blood sugars, they are not getting nutrition to the brain. Their thinking is muddled and foggy. They may not remember what they are supposed to do. They may not have the coordination to open their juice or unwrap their granola bar. They need help. Also remember to explain that it only takes a few minutes to recover from a low blood sugar if the kid gets some carbohydrate in a hurry. No need to make a big deal, just help him get something to drink or eat.

I asked them to call me any time they felt they needed to. I would be available by phone at all times, and I would be grateful if they called me, no matter what. "When in doubt," I said, "please call me. I want to take the best possible care of my child, and I appreciate your help."

Tip: If you cannot be available, give teachers someone to call who can help your child.

Late for School

I explained to the teachers every year, that if either Spike or Bo were experiencing a very low blood sugar in the morning, I might have to keep him home for an hour or so while we worked on balancing his body chemistry. Or, if we were having a rough night of highs and lows, he might not get his homework finished. My boys were late to school several times throughout their school careers due to their numbers (blood sugar levels). I always dropped in on their teachers or called the school (in the later years) to let them know that we were doing the best we could to control their blood sugars. We always told the school when there was a blood sugar problem. We never ever used diabetes as an excuse unless it was a diabetes-related problem that kept the kid home.

Remember, you want your child to thrive. He can do anything with diabetes. Sometimes you just have to take a little time to get things back into balance. The authority figures you deal with will need gentle reminders about this from time to time.

The Cooler

We packed emergency Coolers (Little Playmate) with Gatorade, graham crackers, Goldfish, jerky, peanuts, candy, and frosting. One packed cooler was placed in the office. One packed cooler was placed at the teacher's desk. In addition, Spike and Bo both carried a cooler to school packed with snacks and their lunch **every day**.

Tip: Tape a copy of the low blood sugar Symptoms inside the top of each Cooler.

Plastic Reclosable Bags

I asked teachers to carry the bag of supplies for treating low blood sugar on bus rides, field trips, and during **fire drills**. The boys would also carry their Coolers. The teachers and office had my emergency phone number and called me whenever Spike or Bo was low.

Substitute Teachers

If you drop your child off at school, check and see if there is a substitute teacher. You will need to talk with each substitute teacher. Tell her that your child has diabetes. Show her the Symptoms printout. Tell her that your child may need to eat in class, go to the restroom, or check his blood sugar and may need help. Ask her to call you if there is a problem and show her the plastic bag with emergency supplies in the teacher's desk. Be prepared to give her a plastic bag of her own.

If your child takes the bus to school, then you need to give your child's teacher a set of instructions, printed out, that she can leave for a substitute teacher. Let your child know that if there is a problem, he can phone home, and you will come to the school and help.

The School Bus Driver

Take the time to introduce yourself to the school bus driver. Let her know your child has diabetes. Tell her you don't expect your child to have any problems on the bus ride to and from school, but, just in case, give her a copy of Symptoms and a plastic bag containing juice, a granola bar, and a tube of frosting.

Grade School Snacks and PE

You can really help your young child if you work with his teacher in scheduling his snacks and PE. If there is a choice, PE should be after snack or lunch. If not, your child will probably need a special small snack before or during PE, like some crackers and juice. And then you need to be ready for the unexpected. When

Bodie was in the first and second grade, he looked like an angel, so he rarely got into trouble, but he was a very active little boy. On a few occasions, as a form of discipline, his teacher had him sit on the bench during recess. This didn't work well for Bodie. His blood sugars soared, making him feel even more restless. I very calmly explained to his teacher that Bodie **relied on exercising** at 10 AM, noon, and again at 2 PM to help lower his blood sugar. She understood, and together we figured out a plan that worked better for Bodie. From then on when she wanted to discipline Bo, she asked him to run a lap. Her message got across, and his blood sugar did better.

Preparing for Emergencies

With children dependent on a constant flow of insulin and carbohydrate, you have to think things out. Basically, life needs to be arranged, so they are never separated from their kits or their food—that means in fire drills, traffic jams, field trips, and emergencies.

Fire drills. Fire drills are routinely conducted at schools, but once in a while the kids may be kept lined-up outside their classrooms for extended periods of time. To prepare for this, ask your child's teacher to carry the plastic bag you have given her during **every fire drill**. Your child should also be allowed to carry his cooler during fire drills.

Traffic and car trouble. Believe it or not, getting stuck in traffic can quickly turn into an emergency situation. To avoid this problem, always have a packed cooler in your car. When your child goes in a car with friends, he should carry a cooler. The cooler should be on every bus, in every van, and on every field trip.

Earthquakes, mud slides, and storms. We live out in the country and there have been many times when Spike and Bo could not get home from school because of heavy rains and mud slides. Our road was closed just this past December by a fire. In anticipation of this, we made a plan. At the beginning of the school year, we decided which friend's house in town they would go to should the roads be closed. This way they would be safe, and I would know where to find them. We chose a friend whose mother knew the boys and understood their need for insulin and carbohydrate. I left a permission slip at the school. As an extra precaution, I went to the local drug store and made arrangements for the boys to be able to walk in and pick up all their diabetic supplies if their kits were lost or stolen. (I did this when they were very young.) In addition, the boys always have their kits and coolers with them. (If they go to school or to a friend's house and forget their kit or cooler, I immediately drive over and drop off their supplies.)

Bullies

Sometimes kids run into a bully, someone who is habitually cruel or plays on others' vulnerabilities. A bully can be a student or an adult. Diabetes is a tough condition to handle. It takes a brave kid to do it well. When it was a kid doing the bullying, I let Spike and Bo handle it. When an adult in a position of authority behaved in a mean-spirited manner or made diabetes-related fun of one of the boys, I stepped in. My first approach was to ask the adult to help me take care of my child. Then I shared information and educated the adult. If kindness didn't prevail, I went to that person's boss. We have always been able to stop cruel behavior.

Spike had an interesting experience in the fourth grade with a kid who tormented him once too often. Spike was little, the smallest kid in his class. He was also the youngest kid in his class, and he was smart. During the early years of dealing with diabetes, he avoided all sweets, cake and ice cream included. A classmate had an ice cream party to celebrate her birthday. A big fourth grader grabbed a giant bowl of ice cream and cake, walked up to Spike and said, "Ha ha, you can't have ice cream." Spike tells me that is the only time he ever cried at school. It really hit a nerve.

"What did you do?" I asked, my heart sinking.

Spike said, "I grabbed his hand and shoved the bowl right into his face."

The rest of the kids cheered. The bully quit tormenting Spike. In fact, today Spike and that kid are friends. Spike's reaction may be a little too physical for some kids. But if someone is bullying your child at school, help your child be brave and go to his teacher and have the bullying stopped.

Go to Your Child's School

I am a stay-at-home mom, and I wanted to be with my boys as often as possible and handle as much of their care as I could. This is my parenting style; it worked for us. If at all possible, try to be at home with your child and help him with his diabetes, at least during the early years.

When the boys were in grade school, I went to the school every day at 10:00 AM and noon to do the boys' blood tests. I would quietly walk into class and matter-of-factly do a finger prick and then read the blood sugar number. This was interesting because every time I went to school to do a blood test on Spike or Bo, a few kids would gather around to watch and ask questions. Sometimes the students would read the blood sugar number and help decide whether a snack or maybe a little insulin was needed. (The entire procedure takes about 2 minutes.) I think the students' involvement and understanding of Spike and Bo's diabetes and how hard they tried to control it resulted in a lot of informed, compassionate young people.

After all these years, kids love to come to our house and sit around and tell stories about the time they helped Spike when he was low on the playground, or the time one of the boys helped Bo paddle in when he got low while surfing. Given a chance to fulfill the expectation by adults of caring behavior, your child's friends will become your child's advocates. I always trusted the boys' friends to notice when they were down, to give them a sugar drink or candy, and to call me. They have never let me down.

A NOTE TO PARENTS FROM SPIKE

When I was young, I always imagined myself to be a very independent kid. I didn't want my parents to tell me what to do, and I certainly didn't let my big sisters get away with bossing me around. But in one area, even if I acted like I could handle it on my own, I was certainly glad that I didn't have to go it alone. I was so grateful to my parents for giving me my injections, planning my meals, or checking my blood sugars during soccer games. I didn't necessarily let on to it. I said, "I'm 10 years old Dad; I don't need you telling me to drink more Gatorade." Thank God he told me.

There was always someone there, whether it was Mom, Dad, Mary, or Jenny. Even Bo looked out for me, even if I

continued

told him "Whatever Bo, I'm not crying because I'm low. . . ." Anyway, I don't think kids should be pushed to grow up fast when diagnosed at an early age with something as significant as diabetes. There will come a time when your kid just says, "No thanks Mom, I'll be giving my own shots now." (Except when I am sick—then she can still do it, and I'm 19.) You'll know when it's time for your kid to take over; he'll tell you.

Looking back, while I was growing up I was glad my parents were there taking care of the adult stuff, the diabetes, even if I didn't let on.

The Law

The rights of children with diabetes are protected by law: Section 504 of the Rehabilitation Act of 1973 and the Americans with Disabilities Act. You'll work together with the teachers and principal to develop a Section 504 medical treatment plan for your child. The plan should meet your child's need for snacks in class, extra drinks of water and bathroom breaks, and time for blood sugar checks and administering insulin. You'll probably also include treatment for high and low blood sugars and special times to watch for them.

5

Exercise and Sports

Exercise is one of the three important elements in managing diabetes. It follows insulin and carbohydrate. The food we eat turns into glucose (sugar) in the bloodstream. Insulin allows sugar to get into the cells to be used for energy. Without insulin, the sugar just piles up in the bloodstream. But there is another way that sugar can get into cells without insulin. Exercise opens a second path. The easiest way to explain this phenomenon to kids, teachers, and coaches is this: When you exercise, your muscles warm up; warm muscles absorb sugar; very warm muscles—muscles taken to the point of exhaustion—absorb a *lot* of sugar. **The normal, everyday playtime activities of children help to keep their blood sugars level.** On sick days, or very quiet days, or especially during long car rides, you will notice your child's sugars go up. You will need to lower the carbohydrate intake, or give a little extra short-acting insulin, or make sure there is time for exercise.

Make Exercise Part of the Family Routine

When we figured this out, we made exercise part of our family's daily routine. I mean we *really* made time for exercise. The boys were always in an after-school sport. Of course that meant I had a lot of practices to go to, but it was fun. When team sports were out of season, we did something every day, like bike riding, swimming, surfing, hiking, playing basketball in the driveway, motorcycle riding—you have so many choices.

Tip for Mom and Dad on Getting Your Child to Exercise. Exercise Together.

In the process of raising four kids, I noticed that kids don't automatically go outside and exercise because *you* tell them to. They go outside because you are outside. They want to surf because you are surfing. Rick or I went outside and played with the boys or took them someplace to play or to practice sports or surfing every day. That means Saturday and Sunday, too. Even when they were older and had a lot of homework, exercise was part of our daily routine. I like to tell my kids, "We all have jobs. Your dad's job is to go to work and make money. My job is to raise you kids. Your job is to go to school and be a kid. Part of being a kid

who feels well is insulin, eating, and exercise." You have to work to really make exercise part of your daily routine, but the payoff is tremendous.

Weekdays Versus Weekend Exercise

Exercising twice a day helps keep blood sugars level. At our house we exercise at around 10:00 AM and again at 2:00 PM. During the school week, recess and PE would take care of one exercise session. I always made sure we did something outside right after school.

On the weekend you may have to make a conscious effort to help your child remember to and want to exercise in the morning and again in the afternoon. That's why Spike and Bo played youth league soccer every year, Little League baseball, and basketball. When they weren't on teams, we swam, surfed, played soccer in the driveway—you name it, we played it.

When you figure out how to do sports and balance insulin, carbohydrate, and exercise, your child will be able to achieve whatever level of excellence he desires. Both Spike and Bo were All-Star soccer players every year. So don't spend your time worrying, just get organized.

Have a Little Fun!

I love the ocean, so for our daily exercise we often went to the beach where we could all swim and boogie board, and play in the water close to shore. This all changed when the boys were around ten because they decided they wanted to surf. Surfing took them further out into the ocean. Two boys with diabetes, way out in the ocean, me on the shore watching. . .well, it just didn't work for me, so I got a surfboard and joined the boys. Of

course their sisters, Jenny and Mary, also took up surfing. Their dad, Rick, was always a surfer. I was no youngster when this surfing bug hit our boys. They learned quickly. It was really hard for me to learn, but I kept trying.

Bonding

Surfing became a passion with our boys. Sitting out there with the boys and their friends is the most fun thing I have ever done in my life. Of course I carried a frosting stuffed into the sleeve of my wet suit. I was close to the boys when they were little in case they got low, and we were having a blast. Making exercise a part of the family's routine will bring your family closer together.

We have found that being in water, especially cold water, takes special precautions when you have diabetes. In the boys' book, and on their web site, Kidsanddiabetes.com, they give specific guidelines for surfing. Basically, you lower the insulin you take before surfing, eat a big meal before going out into the water, carry frosting or glucose gel in the sleeve of your wetsuit, come in every hour for food, and **never surf alone.**

Tip: We have found that following strenuous exercise, warm muscles absorb sugar for 4 to 8 hours. After a hard day of exercising, the nighttime dose of short-acting insulin is usually lowered. You might lower the dose by half or even take only ¼ dose. In some cases, they may take no short-acting insulin at night.

Enlisting their Friends' Help

When the boys grew older and began to go to the beach without me, I gave a speech to their friends *every time*. Before they would leave the house, Spike and Bo would say, "Okay, mom, give your speech."

This is what I would tell their 15- or 16-year-old friends, *every time*! "Okay, you guys, you know Spike and Bo have diabetes. They get low sometimes. If you ever see Spike or Bo acting listless on his surfboard, paddle into shore with him. When you get to shore, give him Gatorade. If Spike or Bo gets into trouble out in the water, grab his frosting from the sleeve of his wet suit and give it to him. Ask other surfers for help. Get him to shore. You know Spike and Bo are supposed to paddle in every hour for a snack. Please paddle in with them. They are probably going in because they are tired or a little low. Remember guys, if there's a problem, if Spike or Bo starts to pass out, squirt the frosting between his cheek and gums."

What did this request for responsible behavior do to the boys' friendships? Spike and Bo's best friends are the guys they surf with. A special bond has formed with this group of young men. They really care about my boys, and they have come through and helped on several occasions.

Cute Surf Story

I guess my harping on what to do when Spike or Bo are low stuck with the boys they surf with, but you'll see why it's good to repeat the guidelines. One afternoon after a surfing safari, a gang of boys drove up to the house, sunburned, sandy, surf-boards thrown in the back of their pick-up trucks. Spike led the pack as he stomped into the house. "How was the surf?" I asked, "Catch anything?" Spike didn't answer my question, he said, "Mom, what have you been telling Spencer?"

"I don't know what you're talking about, Spike. What's up?"

Spike went on to tell me that while they were sitting out on the lineup (that's when all the surfers sit on their boards, out in the water, waiting for a set to come in), they got to talking about what they would do if Spike or Bo crashed out in the ocean. Kevin said he'd grab him, put him on his board, and pad-dle in. Somebody else said he'd go find somebody on the beach with a beer. Spencer said, "Don't worry, Spike, if you pass out on your board, I'll pee in your mouth."

"Spencer," Spike replied. "I'd rather drown."

All the boys were standing around in the kitchen while Spike told me this story. "Spencer, Spencer!" I said, "You pee on a jellyfish sting. When Spike's low, he needs sugar!"

"Oh," he said.

One of our favorite stories!

SPORTS

Team sports provide the perfect solution to putting exercise into your child's daily schedule. Exercise helps lower blood sugar. You are going to learn to love all sports activities! Each sport will require a little fine-tuning of insulin and carbohydrate. Basically, the more strenuous the sport the lower the sugar. So many kids play soccer that it's a good sport to look at closely. When Spike and Bo were little, I went to every practice, did blood tests at the quarter or halftime, and gave them their snacks. Here is how we handled team sports.

Talk to the Coach

First, I printed out a copy of Symptoms (page 174) for the coach and assistant coach. At the first practice, I met with the coach and said something like: "I would like you to know that Spike has diabetes. He is a wonderful athlete, but he has to eat snacks and drink Gatorade about every 15 minutes when he is running a lot. Spike will always have his extra snacks here in his cooler. I have printed out some information for you. Sometimes when kids have diabetes, their blood sugar gets very low. When they are really low, their brains aren't getting any sugar, and their thinking gets a little foggy. If Spike ever seems different, very tired or a little out-of-it, ask him to drink some Gatorade. He has never passed out at a sports event, but I think we should be prepared for the worst-case scenario. So, I have a plastic bag here with juice, a granola bar, and a tube of frosting. Please put this baggie in your sports bag, just in case. If Spike ever passes out, put all the frosting between his lip and gum. Just let me know if you have any questions."

From that point on when Spike or Bo would practice and play in games, every 15 minutes or so they would run over to the sideline for a swig of Gatorade, and then play on. **They always ate a substantial snack at halftime,** like half a peanut butter sandwich, crackers and Gatorade, or Chicken McNuggets and Gatorade. This routine made playing team sports work for us.

Other Kids' Reactions

Bodie had a hilarious thing happen to him during his second baseball season. This goes to show you that you never know what kids are thinking. Spike and Bo both played baseball. I'd run back and forth between games, checking sugars, handing out snacks, taking care of my boys. The girls were in sports too, so we were busy, and I didn't always have time to get all their snacks packed before we took off down the mountain. Baseball games often started around five o'clock and went through the dinner hour. At the time, the boys were taking regular insulin and NPH. They needed their insulin injections sometime during the late afternoon. Regular would kick in within 30 minutes, and NPH would overlap with the regular 2 hours after injecting. So, exactly 2 hours after a shot, they would need a big snack. They liked Chicken McNuggets, so Chicken McNuggets it was. We got a routine going so on the way to a game, we'd stop at McDonalds and pick up two boxes of McNuggets, head out for the game, shoot up, play for two hours, and then I would hand them their snack. This was our routine. It worked. They were always eating McNuggets around the 7th inning.

One day after a game a cute little boy came over to talk to Bodie. He had been watching all this. The diabetes didn't faze the boy, nor the shots, but he was concerned about Bodie's diet. "Is it true," he asked Bodie, "that all you and your brother can eat is Chicken McNuggets?" Bodie was only eight, but he explained to the little boy that he had to eat during games; Chicken McNuggets were just his favorite thing to eat. What a wonderful little boy to be so concerned about Bodie.

Tip: If you use a mixture of regular and NPH, your child needs a snack two hours after injecting.

Protect your Child from Interfering Adults

Sometimes you will find yourself blithely going about your business, doing blood tests, handing out snacks, meeting your kid at the side of the field with a bottle of Gatorade, and you'll feel the stare of a disapproving parent drilling into your back. At first, when I was very young and the boys were very young, this bothered me and made me feel a little bit defensive. But the disapproving glares only came from adults ignorant of the facts. Instead of getting mad at these people, I decided to be nice. When I would give my child a snack no one else on the team was eating, I'd simply tell the folks in the vicinity, "Bo has diabetes. He takes insulin and must have 40 extra calories every 15 minutes when he is playing sports." End of problem. In fact, by sharing that information, now we had another family on our team watching out for Bo.

That's another reason it is so important for everybody to know that your child has diabetes, so they can help. Given a chance, most people will react with consideration and compassion. An additional benefit comes from everyone knowing. People in the community often tell me how proud they are of Spike and Bo because of how well they conduct themselves, "even with diabetes."

When the boys were six and seven, Spike was playing right forward. He was a great soccer player, a good runner, and at that time he needed a lot of extra calories. During one game, I had given Spike his Gatorade for the third time when a woman ran all the way around the end of the field to give me a piece of her mind. She had pinged on me. I watched her steaming over. She just had to say in a huff, "You know if you would just leave your son alone and quit interfering he would be a lot better off."

"No," I said to her in my kindest voice, "Spike has diabetes. He takes insulin, and he needs extra calories, about 40 every 15 minutes. That's why I stand on the sideline with a bottle of Gatorade, so he can play sports like every other kid."

"Oh, I didn't know," she said.

"Well, now you know. We are just doing the best we can."

Balancing Insulin, Food, and Exercise

Each day as you cook breakfast, you will think about balancing the amount of insulin you are going to give your child with food and exercise. You will get the hang of it. This means that you will be adjusting the amount of short- or rapid-acting insulin (regular or Humalog) to the amount of carbohydrate and the amount of exercise you expect to occur, or the exercise your child has just had. For instance, school days tend to be routine. In grade school, kids go to school around 8 AM, snack at 10 AM, play at recess after snack, return to the classroom until lunch, play after lunch, return to the classroom, and then exercise again after school, around 2 PM. Once the schedule is established, you'll be giving the same amount of insulin each day, until something changes (they grow, get a cold, or the weather gets real cold.) **Adjusting insulin to fit with carbohydrate, exercise, and change is what you are going to learn to do.**

Every Day is Different

You may do everything the same one day, same insulin, same food, same routine, and the next day your child's sugars are all out of whack. When this happens—and it will—you need to help your child decide what to eat and whether or not he needs extra insulin. Why does this happen? To help you figure out why, there is a checklist you'll want to run through in your mind when you've given the same amount of insulin as yesterday but your child has wildly high or low sugars.

- Did he eat all his breakfast? Was his food intake a little different?
- Did he exercise at a different time?
- Was something exciting or stressful going on at school? A party, a test?
- Is the insulin good? (We throw opened bottles of insulin away after six weeks.)
- Is he getting sick? (You will begin to be able to anticipate when your child is coming down with a cold or flu, because his sugars will go sky high.)
- Is he growing? When they are growing, their sugars are usually higher and harder to keep level.

If you can figure out what was different, then you will be able to balance insulin, carbohydrate, and exercise tomorrow. If you can't put your finger on what caused the high or low sugars, then make an adjustment to fit the situation, and the next day, start all over again. You may want to do an extra blood test the following day at the trouble time to help make adjustments to food and insulin. **(When you are learning to adjust the amount of insulin you give your child, make small adjustments, one unit at a time.)**

When You Give Extra Insulin

You will probably discuss giving extra insulin with your doctor before you get the courage to vary your child's usual dose. Once you begin to adjust insulin daily—when you see very high blood sugars of 240, 320, or more—you will probably want to take care of that high with units of rapid-acting insulin. When your child is very small, you will be in constant contact with your doctor about adjusting his insulin and giving extra, very small doses. But the reality is, parents help their children deal with high blood sugars by giving them extra insulin.

Before giving extra insulin, think about the insulin that is already in your child's system. Humalog acts very fast; regular insulin has finished peaking in 3 hours but can be in the system for 8. NPH kicks in 2 hours after injection, peaks 4–6 hours after injection, and then tapers off. Ultralente or glargine maintains a constant flow of a small amount of insulin for 12 hours. You'll need to get to know your insulin. If you are giving extra insulin, think it through. When you see high blood sugars (above 240) if both types of insulin have already kicked in, you may want to give an extra dose.

How Much Extra Insulin?

Our endocrinologist gave us a chart showing that each unit of regular insulin takes care of approximately 40 points of blood sugar. So if it's the middle of the day, mild exercise is expected, the kid is showing blood sugar of 240, and dinner is two hours off, you might want to give 2 units of short- or rapid-acting insulin.

Each child is different. Each child reacts to insulin differently. We could be pretty casual about adjusting Spike's insulin. He would just go along absorbing what we gave him. Bo, on the other hand, reacts quickly to insulin, and hard. Bo would have to be very high before we would give him extra insulin. Until he was a teenager, Bo was not able to take extra insulin at night. As the boys grew and their body weight increased, we were able to give more frequent extra doses of insulin. During puberty, it was common for them to take at least one extra shot a day.

You will want to talk to your doctor about this, but when the kids were small, say younger than 12 or so, we **never** gave more than 2 extra units of insulin at night (to avoid low blood sugar in the middle of the night). Kids need a nighttime snack of protein and carbs to keep their sugars up throughout the night.

Note: Insulin action changes due to the presence of anti-insulin hormones when you wake up. You become more insulin sensitive throughout the day. Here's a rule of thumb:

Morning: One unit of rapid-acting insulin takes care of 30 points of blood sugar.
Afternoon: One unit of rapid-acting insulin takes care of 40 points of blood sugar.
Evening: One unit of rapid-acting insulin takes care of 50 points of blood sugar.

Tip: Always have a bedtime snack.

Tip: Always follow insulin with a small snack, even when they are high. Kids are more comfortable when their sugars come down gradually.

WHEN FRIENDS COME OVER TO PLAY

Spike and Bo have always had bunches of friends over to the house to play. Now that they are older, they don't call it playing but it's the same thing. You can help your child's friends understand diabetes and create caring friendships by including those friends in helping your child. When kids come to your home, give them some guidelines. (This goes for siblings' friends, too.) You will have to repeat your instructions every time somebody comes over. You'll know they get the message when they say, "Yes, Mrs. Loy, I know, don't drink the 7-Up, it's Spike's emergency supply!"

Every time kids come over I show them the snack cupboard and tell them: "These snacks are for Spike and Bo. We need these candy bars, crackers, frosting, and real 7-Up for when the boys are low. You can eat and drink what you want, but do not touch the 7-Up, do not drink the last Gatorade, do not eat the stuff on this shelf." It always worked—except for Erik and the frosting. He never touched the Cake Mate tubes, but he sneaked the chocolate tub frosting. I always knew when Erik had been over because not only did he eat the chocolate frosting, he'd hide the container in the back of the cupboard. It became a running joke. I simply bought another tub and kept it hidden behind the cereal, away from Erik.

Snack Time at Home

Spike and Bo ate every two hours, like clockwork, when they were little (ages 6–12). They were so active that this was the only way we could keep them going. When their friends would come over for the day, say on a Saturday to swim all day, there would be a lot of snacks. Every two hours, I made snacks for everybody; Spike and Bo's snacks were just more elaborate. They might have crackers and cheese and milk. The other kids might not want milk. Many times I did not have enough cheese or hot dogs to feed six extra kids four times that day. In those cases I'd just walk out to the pool with two hot dogs and say, "Guys, Spike and Bo have to have a quick snack. I'm out of hot dogs, sorry." This never caused a problem. The kids respected Spike and Bo's need to eat every two hours. In fact, my boys ate so frequently that often when they snacked the other kids weren't hungry and didn't want any.

Snack Time at Friends' Houses

This is another important point about snacks. Spike and Bo always carried their daily snacks in their coolers. When they were at a friend's house, or at the beach, or on a bike ride, I would tell their friends every time, "Don't drink Spike's Gatorade. He may need it if he gets low. No matter what don't eat Spike's snacks. Okay?" The kids have always been helpful and stayed away from the boys' coolers.

When Spike and Bo were little and visited at their friends' homes, I sent a packed cooler including brown paper bags with the snack time written on the bag. If their friend's mom prepared snacks— great! They might go an entire day without getting into their coolers. But, by sending what they needed, it made it easier on the other mom, and I could relax knowing my boys had what they needed.

Tip: If you give your kid's friends enough information, and allow them to help, they will become your child's best allies.

Sleepovers

The same goes when your child stays overnight with a friend. I would send a cooler packed with food for a day and a half. Many families eat a bowl of cereal for breakfast. Cereal and skim milk isn't enough for a child with diabetes. He needs protein for breakfast. When you send beef jerky or string cheese in his cooler, your child can easily have the protein he needs. I would often leave a quart of whole milk and a pound of bacon off when my boys spent the night. We found that whole milk worked for lows as well as lasting longer in their systems than low-fat or 2% milk.

To tell you the truth, I am very friendly with the families my boys hang out with. I would often call the other mom and ask her, "What's on the menu for dinner. How about breakfast?" These moms were delighted to try to prepare well-balanced dinners and breakfasts. They wanted to help. I got some interesting reports back from their sons about the great breakfasts they had when Spike and Bo were over.

7

Junior High School

When your kids get a little older, you will need to meet with their principal and all of their teachers, just as you did for grade school. How they carry their supplies may change. When my boys entered junior high school, they stopped carrying coolers and put their supplies in their backpacks.

Meet with the Staff

We were able to meet all the teachers together at one big meeting. We all sat down at a long conference table, and I went through the very same process I had gone through each year at grade school. This time there were six teachers to ask for help. I left two packed coolers at the school, one for Spike to put under his favorite teacher's desk and one to be left in the office. I gave each teacher the printouts of Symptoms and What Everyone Needs to Know so They Can Help (pages 177). Each teacher and the attendance secretary was given a plastic bag containing a tube of frosting, a can of apple juice, a granola bar, and a printout of Symptoms. We talked about low blood sugars, eating in class, blood tests, extra insulin, the need to go to the bathroom, and the need to call home. As a result of this meeting, the boys ate in class whenever they needed to and did their blood tests at their desks whenever necessary. Spike and Bo were always treated with compassion and dignity at their junior high school. I believe it is partly due to the groundwork we did as a family before they entered junior high school. I also believe it has a lot to do with their wonderful principal, Jim Berube. Jim called the teachers together, asked how they could help, offered his help, and kept an eye on my boys. Heaven must have sent us Mr. Berube.

Things change when your children go to junior high school. All of a sudden, they become more independent. Spike was our third child going off to junior high school but my first child with diabetes to do so. Our grade school was a mile from the house, and I went there every day. It seemed very natural because our local grade school provided the social life for our rural community. All the moms were there every day, before and after school, chatting and making plans for their kids to play.

The junior high school was down the mountain. The kids rode the bus. I was a basket case the first morning Spike left the house to catch the bus. He was so little. He had to take care of so much. The walk to the bus was half a mile. I really wasn't sure what I was going to do about Spike being down the hill at junior high school. I still needed to be at his little brother's school each day to help Bo with his routine. Spike cleared it up for me at 6:50 AM his first morning of junior high school. He had his backpack packed with everything that he used to carry in his cooler. He had walked out the front door and passed under the oak tree, headed for the secret trail, when he turned around and said, "Mom, I don't want to see your face at my school today. I'll be fine."

"Okay," I answered. I didn't check on Spike. He was fine. He was prepared, the school was prepared, his teachers knew what to do. By the time Bo went off to junior high school two years later, we were all relaxed about it.

NOTE TO PARENTS FROM BO

Your child will probably have some blood sugar fluctuations at the start of school. I discovered some helpful information in a psychology class at Nordhoff High School, which helped explain why kids with diabetes have so much trouble with their blood sugars when they go back to school—change in exercise, change in brain use, and high emotions.

Exercise uses glucose. When you go back to school, your routine is changed. Generally there is a lot less exercise, but exercise lowers blood sugar and helps keep it level. So your levels may be higher.

The brain uses glucose. Brain activity—studying, reading, concentrating on what the teachers say, memorizing, playing intellectual games like chess, stress and nervousness, and intense thinking about and during tests—uses huge amounts of sugar, causing lower blood sugar, even crashing.

Sharon Begley, in *Your Child's Brain* points out that the optimum windows of opportunity for learning last until about the age of 10 or 12: "This was determined by measuring the brain's consumption of its chief energy source, glucose. (The more glucose it uses, the more active the brain.) **Children's brains gobble up glucose at twice the adult rate from the age of four to puberty."**

continued

> **Tip: Kids will need to snack during the course of the academic day.**
>
> **Emotions use glucose.** For all kids, being thrown into a new group causes anxiety and excitement. They will be using more glucose during times of excitement, such as the anticipation of something exciting like a field trip to Magic Mountain.
>
> Spike and I handled bouncing blood sugars by grazing. We kept our coolers filled with trail mix, crackers, Gatorade, beef jerky—whatever we liked to eat—and we snacked all the time.
>
> **Tip: Parents need to let teachers know why their kids need to eat so often.**

Other Kids with Diabetes

Other kids and their families are learning how to manage diabetes. Knowing someone else who is going through the same thing can be very helpful. When Spike was diagnosed (Thanksgiving, 1987), there were no other kids in the area with diabetes. In fact, the doctors told us that childhood diabetes was so rare that statistically Ojai should expect no more diabetics. Spike was it. The next year, 1988, Bo was diagnosed. As of 1999, there are more than a dozen kids in Ojai with diabetes.

Just after Spike was diagnosed, two things happened that changed our lives. First, the day after Spike came home from the hospital, Gloria Forgea, a nurse, called me. She said, "Virginia, you don't know me, but I heard about Spike. I have a few things I would like to drop off at your house that might help you." That was okay with me.

Gloria came over and gave us a BD Lancet Device, told us about $^3/_{10}$ cc syringes, which are much easier to read, and gave us an Inject-Ease, which made it easier for me to give injections.

The second act of kindness came shortly after Bo came home from the hospital. A woman contacted us who had heard about our two little boys. I don't even remember her name, so I have never thanked her, but she changed our lives. She showed up at our front door with her great big muscle-bound 15-year-old son. She said to me, "I know how scared you are. I just wanted you to meet my son. He plays varsity basketball and he's a good student." Spike and Bo and I looked him over. "Don't worry," she went on, "they will grow. They are going to be all right!" You never know what it is that is going to help you or your child with the challenges of diabetes. I urge you to connect with other kids and other families to offer them your support and for you to get their support.

The Playgroup

In 1998 I got a call from a mutual friend that a little girl named Bridget had just been diagnosed with type 1 diabetes. She was in the hospital, and her family was in shock. The next day I showed up at Bridget's house and met her mom and dad. They were scared. I started in with some tips and encouragement. I had typed out Symptoms and lots of helpful hints. I told Patty she could do it and that everything would be all right. Patty tells me that that visit helped her gather her composure and get organized. And boy, did she get organized. She started a play-group in 1998 with two kids and their families. In just over one year, the number grew to 70 kids ranging in age from three to 18. Spike and Bo go to the playgroup whenever they are in town. At 17 and 19 years old you might think they are a little old for a playgroup, but their presence has grown into a teen-mentor program. As the oldest kids in the group and the most experienced with handling diabetes, Spike and Bo share information with the younger kids. They are on hand at the monthly meetings in the park to talk with parents and answer their questions. When the little kids play soccer with Bo, or hear about Spike's college adventures, or see Bo drive up in his Chevy Tahoe with his surfboard on top, an unstated but powerful message gets through to them. That message is: You can do this. Everything is going to be all right! (See How to Start a Playgroup on page 153.)

8

High School

Kids are even more independent when they enter high school. By the time Bo and Spike entered high school, they were having very few low blood sugar episodes. This is partly because they weren't constantly growing, so what they ate stayed with them longer and because their doctor changed the kind of insulin they were taking. When Spike was 15 and Bo 13, their doctor explained that she would like them to switch their long lasting insulin from NPH to Ultralente. The hitch here is that for 10 years they had been able to mix their regular and NPH in the same syringe. Ultralente cannot be mixed with regular insulin, which meant two shots at breakfast and two shots at dinner. She wanted them to switch because Ultralente provides a steady, slow release of a tiny bit of insulin over 12 hours. NPH, on the other hand, peaks 4–6 hours after injecting. This peak was giving the boys lots of lows, and they were getting high blood sugars when the regular wore off before lunch. The boys agreed to make the change.

With better control, we didn't feel it was so urgent that every teacher knew the routine on the first day of school. I did go to school and meet with their high school principal, Jack Smith.

Jack couldn't have been more helpful. He sent a note to each of Spike and Bo's teachers. Over the next week or two, I met with each teacher and gave them a copy of Symptoms. I explained how hard the boys try to control their blood sugars. I explained that they sometimes have to eat in class and what to do in an emergency. In every case, each teacher thanked me for letting them know about the boys' diabetes. Many of their teachers have requested copies of the boys' book so they can better understand diabetes.

Tip: It is important to let everyone know your child has diabetes.

Lockers

Many high schools offer lockers for some or all of their students. Before school starts for the year, drop in at the front office and let school authorities know that your child needs a locker for health reasons. Ask for a centrally located locker so your student can store extra snacks: jerky, Gatorade, and his Kit during school hours. (Some schools have Nurse's offices where kids can keep their extra food and diabetes supplies.) Remember that they still need to carry their Coolers everywhere they go.

Tip: Having extra food immediately available will help your child function at school.

Off-Campus Lunch

The reality is kids eat fast foods. You can help your teenager by doing a little homework for him. For instance, if all the kids are

Here's Bo and Grandma Virginia taking his Cooler to graduation.

going to McDonalds for a Big Mac, fries, and a Coke, your kid could have a better fast food meal if he skips the fries (carbohydrates) and drinks Diet Coke. At Taco Bell, three beef tacos (12 carbs each) are better than a bean burrito (55 carbs) during the school day. But, if he and his friends are on their way to the beach for a four-hour surf session, then your child may want to eat a burrito and take a burrito and half a dozen tacos to the beach for a snack. Basically, if it's going to be a quiet day, recommend he skip the fries or at least share them.

Tip: Pick up nutrition guides at the fast food restaurants your child goes to or a book such as ADA's *Guide to Healthy Restaurant Eating,* which has nutrition information for many fast food restaurants.

The School Cafeteria

We introduced ourselves to the woman who manages the school cafeteria. She invited the boys to skip the line and walk right up to the counter for a cookie or milk if they ever needed food in a hurry. They never had to take her up on the offer, but it was reassuring that there was one more person looking out for the boys at school.

After School Activities and Sports

When kids are in clubs or on high school sports teams, you will need to help plan for extra calorie needs during meetings, practices, games, and on the bus when their team travels. Spike and Bo always carried a bottle of Gatorade, granola bars, jerky, and cash in their athletic bags. The coach needs to know that your child may need to test and/or eat frequently during games. Spike and Bo always carried their stocked backpacks or athletic bags with them on the bus.

The parent's job, when kids reach high school age, is to make sure the house is stocked with snack items, Gatorade, insulin and syringes, so your teen can be prepared every day. I used to run through a verbal checklist every morning before they left the house for school: "Got your snacks, your kit, Gatorade, lunch, cooler in your car, some cash? Okay, have a good time."

Some parents think all this preparation is their teen's responsibility. I like to think that I am part of my kids' team. Instead of nagging kids to get ready and get organized, I help them do it. That way they feel less stressed about having to remember all the details. They appreciate the thoughtfulness, and if they leave for school with all their supplies, they will be safe. Making it easier for kids to function happily should be the parent's guiding rule.

Checking In

Once kids get into high school, they often venture off to their friends' houses after school. That was okay with me as long as I knew where they were. Each morning I would ask Bo, "What are you going to do after school?" If he didn't know, I'd say, "If you go to a friend's house, call me and let me know so I won't worry." **Because of the possibility of a low blood sugar, checking-in is a must at our house.**

All Bo had to do was see how scared I got late one afternoon when Spike didn't get home on schedule. I was so worried that Spike had passed out or had driven his truck into a ditch, I grabbed Bo and we jumped into my car to go looking for Spike. Thankfully, he had been at a friend's house and was fine. Both boys hated to cause so much anxiety and after that they always checked in.

If you have trouble getting your teen to check in, tell him this rule and then follow through. **The check-in rule:**

▌ You need to check in with me when you go to a friend's house after school.
▌ If you change your plans, you need to call home and tell me where you are and when you will be home.
▌ If you don't check in and I get worried, I will call every one of your friends and ask them to help me go looking for you.
▌ If it's late at night, I'll also call the police.

I meant it, they knew it, and they checked in!

Tip: A cell phone will make everyone's life easier. The check-in rule still applies. You must know your kids' whereabouts.

Growth Spurts and Puberty

About the time you figure out how to balance insulin, carbohydrate, and exercise, all of a sudden your child's blood sugars will go up. When sugars go up for no apparent reason, there are three things we check for.

▌ **Check for old insulin:** If the insulin is old (has been used for more than 6 weeks), we throw it away and start out with a new bottle. A new bottle of rapid-acting insulin tends to be a little stronger, so be aware.
▌ **Illness:** High blood sugars usually occur when your child is getting sick. If he is coming down with something, you will have to pay close attention to his ability to eat. That means, **figure out what your child is going to eat before injecting insulin.** When kids are sick, they sometimes need more

insulin. We prefer to eat first and then inject accordingly. If the boys need more insulin, we give extra shots throughout the day of short- or rapid-acting insulin.

- **Growth spurts:** Both Spike and Bo went through periods during their teens of being tired all the time, having high blood sugars, and being constantly hungry. You will know when your child is growing because the insulin is new, he's not sick, and still his blood sugar numbers are out of sight.

When kids are growing, growth hormones flood their systems. Growth hormones interfere with the action of insulin. That's why you see the high numbers. You will see many growth spurts throughout the years, but during the years of puberty, high blood sugars are very hard to manage. What usually happened around our house was that the numbers would climb and we would give more and more Regular insulin and extra insulin injections throughout the day. After a few days the daily insulin dose would be up and then the kid would quit growing. You will know this has happened because he will probably have a pretty low sugar. If the food and exercise have been the same and all of a sudden you see very low uncomfortable sugars, you know it's time to lower the insulin dose.

When talking this over with friends in the playgroup, we came up with this observation. When kids are growing, more often than not, parents increase their insulin until they crash. You will be able to avoid most crashes (very low blood sugars) by being patient and slowly increasing insulin doses, by only one unit at a time.

Tip: Don't be afraid to lower the short-acting insulin when you get the sense your child has passed through a growth spurt. When the growth spurt is over, you'll end up giving

a slightly higher dose of insulin. Weight determines insulin need, and your child has grown.

Fixing Type 1 Insulin Resistance

The boys' endocrinologist, Dr. Diana Schwarzbein, explained how to fix insulin resistance in type 1 diabetes to us one day in her office. Both Spike and Bo have found themselves in this condition and both boys were able to regain their blood sugar balance in a matter of weeks. If this happens to your child, you will be able to correct it through diet and insulin, and it's not that hard.

Type 1 insulin resistance is related to growth hormones blocking the action of insulin, in contrast to type 2 insulin resistance, which is a receptor problem caused when cells are filled with too much sugar (energy). Cells need energy. Energy (sugar) is delivered to cells with the help of insulin. Insulin delivers sugar to cells by locking onto cell receptors, like little doors. The insulin comes along and attaches to the receptors, then delivers its sugar. During puberty, growth hormones flood the system. This flood of hormones interferes with the action of insulin; so less sugar is delivered to the cells. During growth spurts, growth hormones increase. When growth hormones increase, insulin should be increased.

Dr. Schwarzbein recommended that the boys increase their daily insulin dose with small amounts of extra short-acting insulin, in our case, regular. For example: Spike might take his usual morning dose of regular (15 units). Then at snack time, if his blood sugar was high (240 or above), he might take an additional 2 units of regular. He would test and take the appropriate amount of short-acting insulin at lunch. Then in the middle of the afternoon, if his blood sugar was high, he

Spike, Dr. Schwarzbein, and Bo

would take an additional 2 or 3 units of Regular insulin (short-acting). There would also be a small increase in bedtime NPH insulin to take care of the dawn phenomenon. One cautionary note here: When the growth spurt stops, it stops all of a sudden. You will have to immediately cut back on the extra insulin or your child will experience some uncomfortable lows.

Tip: Increase short-acting insulin in small steps to avoid low blood sugar.

Insulin resistance can sneak up on you. With Spike and Bo, it occurred during a combination of events. The boys were growing, going through puberty, and they were sick. After a few weeks of high sugars, it seemed like no matter what we did, they were still high. They felt bad, were taking many extra injections of short-acting insulin each day, and had constant high sugars. Dr. Schwarzbein explained to the boys that they were experiencing a rise in growth hormones, which required a rise in insulin.

The treatment. She put Spike on a careful diet. He was hungry and so ate all the chicken, meat, eggs, cottage cheese, and non-starchy vegetables he wanted, but only one serving of carbohydrate per meal. We were very serious about overcoming type 1 insulin resistance with Spike. He came home for lunch for two weeks, and I cooked a T-bone steak for lunch with grated cheese, salad, half a potato or one piece of toast, and lots of water. Each meal and each snack was the same: protein and non-starchy vegetables balanced with a carbohydrate.

Within two weeks, his insulin needs dropped back to normal and so did his sugars. He felt well and was able to get back to his normal routine.

When Bodie was 17, he had a similar experience. He had a terrible case of the flu in November, but was able to keep down food, so he did not have to go to the hospital. He was exhausted and had constant high blood sugars. He slept 15 hours a day, missed school, and felt bad. During December he grew an inch and a half, had tonsillitis, and missed more school. In January he had strep throat, was exhausted, had very bouncy sugars—mostly high—and felt terrible. As soon as the antibiotics knocked out the strep throat, we started on a careful diet just like we had done for Spike two years before.

Bo ate protein, a little carbohydrate, drank lots of water, tested his sugar as many as 10 times a day and took many extra short-acting insulin shots. Again, in a matter of only two weeks, we got his numbers back to normal. (We continued a careful diet for several weeks after that.)

During these difficult times your child will need your help. They can be exhausted from growing or being sick on top of dealing with the tired, achy flu feeling caused by high blood sugar. Bo's sugars fluctuated so drastically during his bout with illness and insulin resistance that he had to come home from school on several occasions. I made a point of visiting his high school teachers, principal, and the attendance secretary to explain the situation. I told them that Bo was struggling with out-of-control sugars, and that as soon as we could get him balanced, he would be back in school. His teachers were patient. This is important because I did not want to add academic stress to his burden. I also spoke with his coach, as he missed several soccer games. Everyone appreciated being informed of Bo's predicament.

Tip: Please let your child's teachers know when things aren't going right. When people know how hard your child is trying to balance his insulin, calories, exercise, and stress, they will be supportive of him.

DR. DIANA SAYS:

Home monitoring has created a wonderful diagnostic tool for people with diabetes. Besides eating well and taking insulin injections, the most important advice I can lend is, "Do routine blood sugar monitoring." On a day to day basis, the only way to know how much insulin is needed is through home blood sugar monitoring. Ideally, blood sugars should be checked before and one or two hours after the start of meals, and again at bedtime. Occasionally 3 AM blood checks are required to distinguish the Somogyi* effect from the Dawn phenomenon. The biggest mistake I see leading to hypoglycemic episodes is when insulin in injected blindly. If nothing else, check before meals and at bedtimes because this is when insulin is going to be injected. Think of your child's blood sugar monitor as your friendly at-home physician. The ability to do blood sugar checks at home is a medical miracle.

Note: If you are having middle-of-the night blood sugar problems, you're going to have to work it out with your endocrinologist.

*The Somogyi effect is a process in which low blood sugar in the middle of the night causes rebound high blood sugar early in the morning. The Dawn phenomenon, in contrast, is a natural process whereby the liver breaks down stored glycogen, dumping sugar into the blood-stream in the early hours of the morning.

9

Traveling the Globe

We have traveled all over the world with both boys. I think some of our routine will help you plan a safe trip. (In Spike and Bo's book, *Getting a Grip on Diabetes*, they go into great detail about what they take on trips, providing tips and lists.) **Parents should carry a second set of everything their child uses to manage his or her diabetes.** If you are traveling with a toddler, each parent should carry a complete set of everything your child needs. By age six, Spike and Bo each carried a backpack with everything. I carried an extra set.

■ Insulin Kit
■ Cooler or backpack with snacks for at least 24 hours
■ Medications in case your child becomes ill
■ Phone number to contact your doctor

Before big trips to out-of-the-way places we would make sure we had all the necessary inoculations. For a foreign country, the boys' endocrinologist recommended that they begin taking Pepto Bismol tablets a few days before the trip and each day while traveling, to help avoid diarrhea.

Sometimes kids don't like airplane food, so I always carried plenty of food in my backpack: a jar of peanut butter, a loaf of bread, a box of Wheat Thins, jerky, peanuts, raisins, cookies, candy, and frosting. During the course of the trip, we never let our supplies run out, constantly replenishing supplies at markets. On one memorable trip, we had car trouble and were stranded in the middle of a rainforest in Costa Rica for almost 24 hours. Everything was okay because the boys had food in their backpacks, and I had lots of food in mine. Their sisters and their dad also carried a bottle of Gatorade, crackers and jerky, so we were set.

Tip: You must never run out of food.

Schedules get thrown off when you travel, so your child will need to test more often. When the routine is broken, it is easy to forget to test, snack, or even inject insulin. It's a good idea to carry a logbook and write everything down. If you think you have injected your child's insulin and just cannot remember (this does happen), wait an hour and do a blood test. If it's sky high, you probably haven't injected.

Just the anticipation of a trip is very exciting. We have seen several low blood sugars during the night before a trip. Once en route, you will have to pay attention because blood sugars can swing high while sitting on an airplane or riding in a car, then drop when you hit the beach or arrive at Disneyland!

Tip: You don't have to treat all the highs. It is worse to be low than high. Excitement can cause a high but wear off before the insulin is done acting.

Tip: If you are new to traveling long distances, work out time zone changes and your insulin schedule with your doctor before you leave home.

The Backpack

This is our checklist for backpacks. Spike and Bo each carried all of the following supplies. I carried an identical backup backpack just in case something got broken, lost, or stolen.

The main body of the backpack contains:

Insulin kit
Gatorade
1 box crackers
1 box cookies
Jerky
Peanuts

Raisins
Snacks packed in
   brown paper bags
Jacket
Hat
Book

The side pocket contains:

Glucagon kit
Frosting
Imodium—for diarrhea
Compazine, Phenergan,
   or Tigan—for nausea
   (Compazine is not for children)

Ketone sticks
Tylenol
Neosporin
Copy of Symptoms

The inside pocket contains:

Passport
Tickets

Money

The large front pocket contains:

Toothbrush
Chapstick
Deodorant
Razor
Swimmer's Ear drops
Sunscreen lotion

Special medical
   supplies, for
   example, asthma
   medication
Pens
Small notebook

Note: Have your kids wear their medical ID bracelet or necklace when traveling.

COLLECTED TIPS

During school, remember: exercise uses glucose, studying uses glucose, the brain gobbles up glucose during heavy concentration, emotions use glucose.

It is important to let everyone know your child has diabetes.

Having extra food immediately available will help your child function at school.

Because of the possibility of a low blood sugar, checking in is a must.

Mom and Dad, *you* put a Gatorade in the front seat of your kid's car!

If you have never gone to an endocrinologist with your child, do it.

Call the doctor when
- You think things are out of control
- Your child is vomiting frequently
- High ketones show and you can't get them down
- Your child has been ill and he tells you he really doesn't feel right

When your child is hospitalized, you need to be there. You need to be at the hospital with your child during surgery and recovery.

Take your child's Kit and Cooler when you go to the hospital.

Let siblings be part of the team.

Always take visual Chemstrips on trips in case of a dead battery or lost meter

10

Driving

Driving is a big deal. Of course, it changes your child's life for the better. When your child has a car, his kit and cooler can always be near him, and everybody can relax. Driving requires some special preparation. You know your child. You and your child will decide when he or she is ready to drive. This is how we got Spike and Bo ready for driving.

We live in the country, so the boys learned how to drive the ranch truck and tractor when they were ten years old. It is important when using heavy equipment that you do not drive with low blood sugar. When the boys were younger and they were going to disc the field or haul hay, we'd check their blood sugar before they drove. They always had a granola bar in their pocket and a bottle of Gatorade with them in the truck or on the tractor. And we agreed that if they even suspected their sugar was getting low, they would stop on the spot, drink some Gatorade, and come up to the house to check their sugar.

The reward for being totally careful about their sugar was they could work for me. Kids want to feel well. They don't want problems. Give your kids guidelines and help them follow them. We discussed blood sugar every time they got on a tractor or into the truck.

Driving at 16

Driving the family car on the highway is a very exciting event and sometimes stressful.

Excitement lowers blood sugars. Stress often lowers blood sugars. When Spike and Bo were learning to drive on the highway, I made a deal with them. "You check your sugar before we drive, and I'll drive with you every day." I always fixed them a snack before we took off on one of our practice sessions, like a roast beef sandwich or BLT and milk.

The Driving Routine

- Test your sugar before you drive.
- Keep a packed cooler in every car.
- **Keep Gatorade on the front seat where the driver can reach it.**

Tip: Mom, Dad, you put a Gatorade in the front seat of your kid's car!

We made a plan for "what to do if you get low." If Spike or Bo felt different, felt high or low while driving, they would pull over, stop the car, and drink some Gatorade. Then they would check their blood sugar. If they were really low, they would have to eat a complete snack and wait 5 or 10 minutes until their sugar came up before driving again.

Learner's Permit

You will be spending 6 months to a year driving with your child before he gets his license. Be consistent. Start the habit of driving with a packed cooler in the car and put a bottle of Gatorade in

the front seat. Make sure your child has eaten before getting into the car. Check blood sugar before driving.

Observe your child while he is driving. Help him recognize signs that he may be getting low. His symptoms of low blood sugar may change over time. When Spike turned 19, he added a new low blood sugar behavior to his repertoire of symptoms. It is one he didn't recognize until it was pointed out to him. Basically, as his sugars fell, he would start talking faster and faster.

We were on a long car trip last summer. Spike was driving when I noticed a subtle change in his speech pattern. I had a hunch his blood sugar was dropping. We were in heavy traffic on the freeway, so I handed him a bottle of Gatorade and asked him to take a sip. We immediately pulled over and grabbed a drive-through burger.

There is a fine line between discussing the practicalities of living with diabetes and embarrassing young people. I always try to be sensitive and positive. After the meal, when Spike was feeling strong again, we talked about this new symptom: talking fast. Since it is an indicator that his sugar is falling rapidly, we decided that he should tell his friends. If they notice that he is talking fast, they should say, "Hey Spike, I think you're low. Drink some Gatorade."

Drivers Training

Kids find behind-the-wheel driver's training to be very exciting and stressful. Spike and Bo both lowered their short-acting insulin and ate huge meals before each driver's training session.

You need to tell the driver's training instructor that your 16-year-old has diabetes. Tell him that you expect your son or daughter to have good blood sugar but that if he needs carbohydrate, he will snack. Feed your child a big meal before his driver's training session. Because it's so exciting, you may want to lower his short-acting insulin before each driving session. Have your teen check his sugar right before he gets into the car with the driving instructor.

11

When Your Kids Drink

We have always discussed drinking with all of our kids. Kids start experimenting with alcohol as early as junior high school, so start talking early. I am very aware of what is going on in my kids' lives and what their peers are up to. So, here's how we handle drinking.

I think the key here is repetition, repetition, repetition. When the boys go out with their friends, I give them the drinking lecture every time.

"Listen you guys. I don't recommend drinking, but if you do, don't drink much. And be sure to eat something, too. Beer is better than hard liquor, but beer is full of sugar. It will send your blood sugar up. Later in the evening your sugar may come crashing down—especially if you haven't eaten anything—and you'll get low. If you drink too much and throw up, you have to call me. I won't get mad. I'll just come and check your blood sugar. If you drink and pass out, someone has to check your blood sugar to see if you passed out from booze or are in a low blood sugar diabetic coma. I love you, and I want you alive. Drinking is serious. If you drink and get into trouble you will need lots of help."

I have given the boys this lecture a hundred times. **This is what I tell their friends, every time they go to a party.** I grab their buddies and say: "Listen, you guys. I don't think Bo is going to drink beer, but if he ever slips up and drinks too much and passes out, he could die. This is no joke. If Bo drinks too much and passes out, you have to promise me you will call me, so I can come and do his blood sugar. I promise I won't get mad. Kids make mistakes. Sometimes they drink too much. It happens. But, we don't want Bo dead. So call me."

Or: "Do you remember when Spike had the flu and threw up and ended up in Intensive Care? Throwing up from beer is like throwing up from the flu. It can be dangerous for Bo! So if Bo drinks too much and throws up, you've got to call me."

Spike and Bo try very hard to keep their blood sugars balanced and so will your child.

But Kids Need to Know Exactly What to Do if They Screw Up. So Do Their Friends.

- If a kid with diabetes passes out: Call home for help or call 911.
- If a kid with diabetes throws up once: Get help.
- If he throws up twice and you can't take his blood sugar: Get help or call 911.
- Please make your kids and their friends feel safe about calling you day or night if they mess up.

Note: Tell your kids about alcohol. Drinking a beer is one thing. Drinking tequila shooters is truly dangerous.

Note: Girls and alcohol. Girls need to know that females absorb alcohol about twice as fast as males. That means girls must pay even more attention to the amount they drink.

Note: Wine or beer has sugar in it. Initially sugar causes a rise in blood sugar. In the middle of the night, a normal function of your liver is to break down stored glycogen to sugar, which makes your blood sugar normal in the middle of the night. But alcohol blocks this natural breakdown of glycogen to sugar, which can cause a very low blood sugar. Eat a bedtime snack.

12

College

Getting ready for college is thrilling. Spike and Bo each have found the college experience exciting, fun, and challenging. There are a few things you can do to make the transition from living at home to living in a dorm safely.

Preparing to Go to College

We visited each college campus Spike and Bo wanted to attend. While on campus, we stopped in at the Students with Disabilities Office and asked for some information and guidance.

Counselors suggested that Spike and Bo register as students with disabilities in case their diabetes caused them to be unable to attend class or take exams. (They each marked the "disabled student" box on their college applications and then registered with the Office of Students with Disabilities upon arriving on campus.)

At most campuses, there are teams already set in place to help students should they need it. We did not expect problems, but the reality of life is that when you're a teenager away from home, illness and accidents happen. In Spike's case, the week before finals in his freshman year, he had a skateboarding accident and broke his elbow. The break required surgery, which required hospitalization followed by several days of very strong painkillers, which knocked him out. Spike was not able to monitor his diabetes during this time, so he needed to be at home. Since he had registered with the disabled students' office, his professors were open and helpful when he asked for an incomplete on his exams. Ten days later, when he was able to return to school, he met with each professor and set up a time to take his finals. Had he missed classroom time, the Office of Students with Disabilities would have had someone take notes in his absence.

Roommates

Most kids go off to college and live in dorms. When we dropped Spike off at Stanford, and two years later when we dropped Bo off at USC, I made a point of talking with their new roommates. You should do the same. Make sure your college student's roommate and the dorm RA (resident assistant) have a little knowledge about diabetes. (I gave them each a copy of *Getting a Grip on Diabetes*.) Basically, I told the roommates that Spike and Bo have diabetes. That means they eat often, test their blood, and take insulin. We don't expect any problems, but if Spike should act a little out of it, fuzzy, or tearful, he needed help. The roommate should hand Spike something to drink or eat. We showed Spike's roommate where he kept his granola bars and emergency frosting.

Emergency Procedure for Roommates

Expect the best, but be prepared for the worst. It's okay to call 911. When in doubt, call 911. I explained that if Spike were ever really out of it, or couldn't wake up, it was an emergency!

Sleeping in the dorm.

His roommate should give him frosting and call on other students to help. (Open frosting and squirt entire tube into his mouth between cheek and gums.) If Spike didn't wake up after having been given the frosting, his roommate could give him a glucagon injection or call 911. We took Spike's glucagon out of his room refrigerator and looked over the vials and syringes, so his roommate would be familiar with the process. We posted the instructions for using glucagon up on the closet door.

Glucagon Instructions: When Do You Use Glucagon?

Inject Spike with glucagon if you can't wake him up or if he is so disoriented he doesn't make sense, and you can't get him to eat.

How Do You Use Glucagon?

1. Inject the liquid in the syringe into the bottle of glucagon powder.

2. Shake the bottle until the glucagon dissolves and becomes clear.
3. Draw all the glucagon solution into the syringe.
4. Inject all the solution into his leg or butt.
5. Put Spike on his side, because when he wakes up, he may throw up.
6. Give food as soon as he wakes up: Gatorade, crackers, cookies, or anything he can eat.
7. **If he doesn't wake up or you are not sure of what is going on, call 911.** Be sure and tell the paramedics that Spike has diabetes.

Things to Do Before Going to College

▪ Visit the college campus.
▪ Visit the Office for Students with Disabilities. Ask for their advice.
▪ Mark the "disabled student" box on your college application.
▪ Enroll in the college student health insurance program even if you already have good insurance.
▪ When filling out housing request forms, make sure you mark special housing needs. Ask for housing on campus and near a food supply. **Send forms in on time!**
▪ Start the Hepatitis B series of inoculations six months before school starts.
▪ Some schools recommend a meningitis vaccination.
▪ Get a flu shot before leaving for college or while on campus.

Prior to Leaving for College, Visit the Campus Again

▪ Locate places to eat, cafeterias, coffee shops, food places that are open all night.

- Locate the student health center.
- Locate the nearest emergency room to your kid's dorm.
- Make an appointment with a doctor at the student health service center before school starts or during the first week of school. Your regular doctor will have your diabetes-related records sent to him/her.
- Have all diabetes-related prescriptions sent to the school pharmacy before school starts. Phone to make sure your prescriptions are in place.

Supplies to Take to College

- A room refrigerator stocked with: insulin, **glucagon**, cottage cheese, whole milk, string cheese, nuts, and raisins.
- A typed list of emergency phone numbers: parents, doctor, endocrinologist, school clinic, adult brothers and sisters. Tape it to the phone.
- Glucagon instruction sheet.
- Symptoms instruction sheet.
- Insulin Kit.
- Ketone test strips.
- Medical I.D.
- Blue Ice cold packs—two.
- Cooler—packed for car trips.
- A huge box of snacks: jerky, crackers, cookies, noodle soup cups, nuts, frosting, candy.
- A second set of:
    Insulin
    Syringes
    Meter batteries
    Blood testing strips or disc
    Chemstrips

Once you have dropped your child off at his dorm, keep in touch. Living away from home, being in complete charge of managing their diabetes, late nights, college food, parties, beer, even buying the expensive diabetes supplies, is a lot to juggle. Both Spike and Bo had some serious low blood sugars during their first weeks at college. When Spike went away to college, I think we left him alone too much. He had a long, hard time getting his blood sugars under control. Spike was handling everything on his own when one evening, after a long day of snowboarding, he miscalculated his insulin needs. He took too much insulin after a day of extreme exercise. He ended up passing out. His roommates called 911, and Spike was revived by paramedics who gave him a glucagon injection.

This experience caused me to be a little bit more involved with Bo during his first few months away from home. When Bo left for college, just like Spike, his numbers were especially hard to get under control. Bo called and e-mailed me many times those first few months away to discuss what he could do to control his blood sugars. Bo saw the doctor at the student health services several times. He came home once to see his specialist who fine-tuned his insulin regimen. We even brought Bo home for the weekend twice that first semester. Over those long weekends at home, Bo was able to get his sugars under control and return to college fortified and confident.

Tip: Make a deal with your college student. Encourage him to phone you day or night to discuss blood sugars, insulin dose, food, anything. Remember, when his blood sugars are out of control, his thinking is a little foggy. A phone call at midnight, a little advice from Mom or Dad, some encouragement, can make a big difference.

Long Distance Help

Sometimes you will need to help your child from a distance. I want to relate an incident that happened to Spike recently and how we were able to handle it together.

3-31-01

2:15 AM: Spike phoned home in the middle of the night. I immediately began writing down what he said. "Mom, this is Spike, I'm vomiting a lot and not doing so good. The first time I vomited I asked two of my friends to keep an eye on me. But I threw up again, and I'm really feeling nauseous."

"What's your sugar, Spike?"

"It's 51. I'm really feeling sick, I can't even keep a sip of Gatorade down. I've got glucagon here. What do you think?"

"I think it's time to inject the glucagon."

"You think I should inject the glucagon?"

"Yes, Spike. It is time to use the glucagon. Do you know how to fill the syringe?"

"Yes."

"Okay, I'll stay on the phone while you get ready. Hey, Spike. Before you inject it, I need the phone numbers of four of your buddies who live in the frat house. Tell me four names and phone numbers of guys who are home now. If you pass out, I'm going to call all of them." Spike gave me four numbers and four names.

"Okay, I'm filling the syringe. How do you get the air out?"

"Just point the needle up and squirt a little liquid out."

"Oh yeah, that works fine."

"Can you inject yourself, Spike, or shall we call a friend?"

"I want to do it. Okay, I'm going to put the phone down and inject the glucagon. Where should I inject it?"

"How 'bout in your leg? Inject it all."

"Okay, here goes."

2:20 AM: Glucagon injection. I listened while Spike injected the glucagon. Then he came back on the phone. "How was it?" I asked.

"Not too bad."

"Listen, if you vomit again it's okay. The glucagon will block your insulin from working, and your liver will release sugar into your system. Hey, Spike, let's talk on the phone while your sugar comes up. Are you watching TV? Me too."

2:38 AM: Blood sugar 124

2:45 AM: Spike was feeling better, not so shaky. He hung up the phone, said he would test and call back at 3:15 AM.

3:10 AM: Blood sugar 130. Feeling okay, a little nauseous. We discussed the insulin he had taken that night, 15 units of regular at six o'clock, right before he ate two burritos, and 15 units of Ultralente. By 3:00 AM the regular was out of his system, and there was just a baseline of Ultralente to think about. The glucagon should keep his sugar up until morning. Spike said he had an eight o'clock midterm. He was going to study for a little while and then get some sleep. He would call back if he was having any anxiety or if he wanted to talk. I said, okay, I'd be up and I would give him a wake-up call at 7:30 AM.

7:30 AM: Spike called. He was okay. He was heading out to take his midterm. If he could eat, he would take a small amount of regular, then sleep. Spike took his midterm, the nausea passed, and he ate a little. He took 5 units of regular and half his Ultralente and slept. He called in the afternoon to say he was sleeping a lot and doing better.

Tip: Each quarter get the phone numbers of four friends who live in the same dorm, fraternity or sorority house as your son or daughter. That way you can call for help should your college student need it.

13

Choosing A Doctor

It is important that you choose a doctor you and your child will be comfortable with through the many contacts you will have. We see a GP (General Practitioner) for everyday stuff like sore throats, earaches, flu shots, and poison oak, and an endocrinologist for diabetes. Our GP encourages the boys' relationship with their endocrinologist. They see their endocrinologist twice a year or more; many kids we know go quarterly.

Taking Your Child to a Specialist, an Endocrinologist

An endocrinologist or pediatric endocrinologist has two years of additional medical training in this specialty. Endocrinologists study the hormones that travel in the bloodstream and have various effects on the body's tissues. Insulin and glucagon are included in these hormones. When planning long-term care for a child with diabetes, you will want a specialist to oversee your child's insulin regimen as he grows and changes.

It takes an expert in the field, an endocrinologist, to make the fine insulin adjustments required for a growing child and/ or a child whose blood sugars are hard to keep level. Some pediatricians specialize in children with diabetes. They will also have the training necessary to monitor your child.

If you have never gone to an endocrinologist with your child, do it. The special expertise these doctors have in managing all aspects of diabetes is remarkable. If you had heart trouble you would go to a cardiologist. If you have diabetes, you should go to an endocrinologist.

Note: According to Dr. Ronald Chochinov, a wonderful endocrinologist practicing in Ventura who donates time to the Kids With Diabetes playgroup: Kids under the care of an endocrinologist don't see complications!

Tip: Your child's relationship with his doctor should be positive. Give yourself permission to change doctors. It must be a good fit.

WHEN YOUR CHILD IS SICK

When your child is sick, you will need to be home because sick days are harder to handle. When kids are sick, they still need insulin. Illnesses usually cause blood sugars to go higher, but when kids are sick their appetite might be off, or they may vomit. This requires a different insulin routine. (It is best if you work out a sick-day plan with your doctor.)

Often when Spike or Bo was sick, we would only use short-acting insulin. We would do a blood test, and then they would eat. Once we were sure they could keep the food down, I would give them short-acting insulin, enough to cover what they had just eaten. They might check their blood sugar and eat and inject 5 or 6 times during the day.

Tip: If your child can't or won't eat or drink, take him to the hospital.

If your child is sick and sleeping a lot during the day, you may need to interrupt his nap, do a blood check, and give him an appropriate snack or a small amount of short-acting insulin.

Ketones

You should have your child check for ketones when he is sick. Just pass a ketone strip through the urine stream. If ketones are present, extra insulin is needed. **(You will want to check with your doctor the first time your child experiences ketones.)** When Spike or Bo produce ketones, they check their blood sugar, then take a small amount of short-acting insulin (2 units), eat a little snack of a few crackers, and drink lots of water. They check every hour. As long as high ketones are showing, they repeat the process: test, take a little short-acting insulin, snack, and drink lots of water until the ketones are gone.

Sometimes you just can't get rid of ketones at home. Dr. Marc Weigensberg, pediatric endocrinologist, explains what happens when ketones build up in the bloodstream. I think his explanation will explain why sometimes a trip to the hospital is necessary. (Regard this as a worst-case scenario, so you'll know how to take steps to prevent ketone buildup.)

Ketones are acids that are produced when your body breaks down fat. If you have high blood sugar, too, ketones mean that you do not have enough insulin in your body to keep fat from breaking down. Your body gets rid of ketones in your urine, so it is important to drink lots of fluids if ketones are present. If ketones are produced more quickly than your kidneys can get rid of them, they will accumulate in your blood and cause nausea and vomiting. It is important to try to get rid of ketones before you get to this point because nausea and vomiting can lead to dehydration and acidosis (too much acid in your blood). This can result in a vicious cycle in which vomiting leads to dehydration, which makes the ketoacidosis worse, which, in turn, causes more vomiting. At this point, you often need to be hospitalized and treated with intravenous (IV) fluids and insulin to break the cycle. The only way to keep ketones from forming is to take extra insulin."

Tip: Always eat a little when you take insulin.

Tip: Anytime your child is not feeling well—whether his blood sugar is high or low—check for ketones. If your child has high ketones, he should let someone know, so they can help.

Note: You can also be in ketoacidosis with low blood sugar, especially after drinking alcohol.

Vomiting

Vomiting can be very difficult to handle. At our house here's how we take care of the problem.

Vomit once:
▌ Sip Gatorade or 7-Up
▌ Check blood sugar frequently
▌ Take small amounts of short-acting insulin (1 or 2 units)

Vomit twice: Call the doctor. Once you have been through the flu or an illness with vomiting a few times (with the help of your doctor), you will figure out how to handle it. Dehydration can happen fast. If it does, you will need to go to the emergency room.

Call the doctor when:
- You think things are out of control
- Your child is vomiting frequently
- High ketones show, and you can't get them down
- You child has been ill, and he tells you he really doesn't feel right

Tip: Take a blood sugar and check for ketones, then call the doctor.

Note: The boys' uncle, pediatrician Martin Berger, has this to say: Your ability to deal with a problem depends on your diabetes comfort zone, which will significantly enlarge as you become more experienced. In the beginning, ask for help whenever a problem with which you're not familiar makes you uncomfortable. At a certain point, these problems will become familiar, and the more frequently you solve them, the more comfortable you'll become. Don't be shy about calling your doctor. Just remember that doctors go through the same process that you do—when they run into an unfamiliar problem, they ask someone who is more expert for advice.

THE HOSPITAL

At our house, we love the hospital. It is like a safety net. When kids get sick, have high blood sugars and ketones combined with vomiting, it may be time to go to the hospital. That's what hospitals are for, to help your child get back into balance. It's all about attitude. Help your kids have a positive attitude about going for extra help. Allow the hospital to be part of your team.

Accidents

When your child is hospitalized, you need to be there. For simple emergency room visits (like a broken arm), take your child's insulin kit and cooler along. You can help the emergency room staff by monitoring your child's blood sugar. In January 1994, Bo got his leg sliced up by a motorcycle chain. It was a nasty accident. We grabbed Bo's insulin kit, put him in the car and rushed off to the ER. I tested his blood sugar on the drive down the mountain, and he was low. I gave him a little Gatorade from his cooler. (We always have a stocked cooler in the car.) During his hour and a half in the ER, while they irrigated the wound and stitched him up, I tested his blood sugar several times. It was painful and scary, and his blood sugar dropped. I gave him little sips of Gatorade and bites of applesauce throughout the process to keep his blood sugar stable.

Spike and Bo tend to have blood sugars that soar right after accidents, then they plummet. You will need to do frequent blood sugar checks after accidents and injuries.

Surgery

You need to be at the hospital with your child during surgery and recovery. It has been our experience that sometimes the hospital staff is familiar with dealing with diabetes and insulin therapy, sometimes they are not. By staying on top of your child's blood sugar numbers, his caloric intake and insulin, you can be very helpful.

During Spike's recent elbow surgery, I took careful notes of his insulin and calorie intake. This information may help you to anticipate the big adjustments made during surgery. Consider your child's weight and normal insulin intake. (You will also get advice from your doctor and the hospital recovery staff.) Spike weighed 150 pounds. The night before surgery, Spike ate a giant steak dinner and took his usual dose of insulin—16 units of short-acting insulin, and 16 units of long-lasting insulin. He did not drink nor eat after midnight. In the morning, he took no insulin and went into surgery about 8:30 AM. Spike was on IV's. The surgery was over at noon. At 3 PM, we checked Spike's blood sugar, and he took 3 units of short-acting insulin. As he was unable to eat for the next 12 hours, he was given glucose in his IV and took only 2 or 3 units of short-acting insulin every four hours. He needed to stay on short-acting insulin for three days following surgery, then long-lasting insulin was added.

Very little insulin was taken the first few days following surgery. It makes sense because he was eating very little.

When your child goes to the hospital take:
▍ Insulin Kit (page 21)
▍ Cooler packed with favorite snacks

COLLECTED TIPS

When there is nothing else in the house, you can always cook scrambled eggs and bacon.

By involving your neighbors, they will become part of your child's team.

To help your child drink lots of water, buy bottled water by the case, little bottles for the little ones, liter sports bottles for teens.

The sooner you make up your mind to always be vigilant, the happier your family life will be.

Do the best that you can each day, and when you make a mistake, try to forgive yourself promptly.

See what your child eats first, then inject the regular or rapid-acting insulin.

Glucose gel can be given during low episodes. Practically speaking, many parents use tubes of cake decorating frosting because they are cheaper, so you tend to keep more tubes around the house, and it works.

Meet with teachers—every single one.

If you cannot be available, give teachers someone to call who can help your child.

You must never run out of food.

When both parents share responsibility, communication between them is essential.

Team sports provide the perfect solution to putting exercise into your child's daily schedule.

14

Parents' Issues

When both parents share responsibility, communication between them is essential! Maybe you will be one of the lucky families where both parents can share the responsibility of handling your child's diabetes equally. But it has been my experience that often the task falls mainly on one parent. Life isn't fair—you already know that if one or more of your kids has diabetes. Life is life. You get what you are dealt, and then you strive to do the best you can with it.

Like all parents of a newly diagnosed child, I was a mess when my two little boys were first diagnosed. I chose to stay home and take care of my boys. Rick went to work each morning and wasn't around during the day to see all the highs and lows, blood checks, snacks, and sometimes tears. In the beginning, I wanted him to take over when he got home from work, to give me some relief. But that really didn't work. It didn't work because I was the one with all the day's information in my head, balancing calories, exercise, and insulin. The evolution of the kids' day didn't stop when their dad got home from work and start all over again. Once I got it out of my head that I needed a break, things went more smoothly at home.

Sometimes, you may need a pep talk to keep focused. I used to sit down and write a list of what was going right. For instance, I have been known to sit down and write a list like this:

- Thank God for blood checks; they allow us to figure out the insulin.
- Thank God for medical science; they invented insulin.
- My boys are alive and well.
- My daughters are caring, compassionate sisters.
- I have finally learned to be organized.
- The kids need a giant breakfast every day. I can do that.
- I can do this!

The Benefits of Preparing Breakfast Every Day

I decided to be the best breakfast chef I could be. No kidding, I have gotten up at 6:15 every school day, a little later on the weekends, for the past 12 years, and cooked a great breakfast. You know what—I love it! The boys love it too. We have a private time together in the morning and talk about their insulin dose. I serve bacon, eggs, fried potatoes, and cheese, double check their supplies, and send them off to school. They are happy because they are cared for; I am happy because my children are prospering.

There are side benefits to doing a good job. Over the years we have had a whole crew of teenage boys show up at our house for breakfast on Saturday and Sunday mornings. Sometimes they would stay and hang out with Spike and Bo to swim, ride motorcycles, go bike riding, or work on their cars. Sometimes they might eat and run. At any rate, they are always appreciative of a mom who cooks.

Another funny consequence of this cooking thing; I have received a dozen phone calls over the years from mothers of the boys' friends. They usually go like this. "Virginia, Ryan says you cook breakfast, bacon and eggs and stuff, for the boys every morning before school. I told him he's crazy."

"It's true, June. I get up every morning and cook a ranch breakfast."

"Well, thanks a lot. Now Ryan wants breakfast before school, too."

SUGGESTIONS FOR COPING

When Parents Don't Live Together

In the case of divorced parents, where your child travels back and forth between parents, communication and planning are vital. If you are separated from your spouse, you know which one of you is the responsible one. If it's you, then forget about what is fair. Do the preparation and planning for your child. Help make her visits with the other parent organized and safe. That means you need to:

▪ Pack her Kit; make sure everything is there, syringes, insulin, glucose monitor, and lancets
▪ Pack her insulin log
▪ Pack her Cooler
▪ Pack extra snacks
▪ If anything out of the ordinary has been going on with her blood sugars, write it down so your ex-spouse can help your child balance her sugars, calories, and exercise.

When children are sick, they need extra care and supervision. This is important. Call a truce with your ex. Make a sick-day plan before it happens. Then when your child is sick, make a call. Say, "Our daughter is sick. I would like to follow the sick-day plan we set up."

There will be many times when your personal plans for the evening or weekend will be interrupted, and you will be needed at home with your child. You can turn this into a win-win situation if you tell yourself and your child: "I chose to be your mom or dad. I want to be here with you and take care of you when you are sick. That's what I do."

Setting Goals to Build Confidence

When diabetes comes to a family, after the initial shock and the initial period of adjustment, Mom and Dad need to sit down and set some goals. We did. We wanted our boys to be able to do anything. An interesting adventure came out of our typically exuberant way of doing things. (You may have read Jenny's version of this story in the boys' book; here's mine.)

The minute Spike was diagnosed, his big sisters learned all about high and low blood sugars, drawing insulin, and where the special low blood sugar foods were located. Even baby Bodie, who was only five years old, knew where the frosting was and walked around the house practicing injecting an orange. Rick and I discussed it and decided it would be a good idea to reward the kids for behaving so well. He suggested a family vacation to Hawaii. "Great idea," I said, "but let's have the kids decide on their reward. Maybe they'd rather go to Disneyland." I was feeling very magnanimous the next afternoon when I gathered the kids together in the living room for a family meeting.

"Listen you guys," I told them, "I'm really proud of you. You remind me of a little army marching around the house taking care of each other. You've all been so wonderful that your dad and I think you deserve a reward."

"Like a pack of gum?" Jenny, the oldest, asked.

"No, I mean a big reward. You guys all like the ocean," I went on, "we were thinking about taking you to Hawaii this summer! Talk it over, see what you come up with, okay?"

The four kids disappeared into the boys' bedroom. Twenty minutes later my angels returned to the living room to announce their plan. "This reward is really for us?" Jenny asked.

"Uh, huh."

"We get to do what we want to do?"

"Yes," I answered, "that's why I suggested a vacation in Hawaii. We can all swim and play on the beach."

"Mom," Jenny went on, "we want to be in the movies!"

"You what?!"

"Yes!" Mary added. "We all want to be in the movies."

"Movies, movies." Bodie chanted.

"It's true, Mom." Spike explained. "That's what we want to do."

Well I ran it by Rick that night. "All right!" he said. "That's a great idea. You figure out how to get them in the movies, and I'll support you every step of the way. Remember, Virginia, we want these kids to believe they can do anything. I think this is a great step in accomplishing that!"

That afternoon began yet another chapter in the lives of the Loy children. We signed them up with an agent, had head shots taken, and for the next three years I drove to LA, sometimes twice a week, so they could do their extra work. Their favorite job, by far, was the day they got paid to ride the roller coaster at Magic Mountain, 33 times!

Stopping Negative Comments from Other Adults

The strangest thing sometimes happens when someone realizes your child has diabetes. Most people are great, they ask questions, nod their heads, show concern. But there are a whole bunch of people out there including relatives, friends, and strangers pushing their carts in the grocery store, who hear the word "diabetes" and then launch into some horror story about their grandmother, uncle, or a kid they went to school with. The first few times this happened I was on overload anyway. I couldn't have been more concerned or scared about my boys. I didn't need to hear about something awful that happened 40 years ago. My boys and your child sure don't need to hear about "complications."

The very first time it happened, I clasped my hands over my 6-year-old son's ears, looked wide-eyed at the perfect stranger who had launched into her story, and said, "Please, don't talk about that around my child." The response was, "Oh, I see, you don't want your child to hear about. . . ," and compulsively, she launched into her negative, scary story again. I am no longer so passive.

When one of my children is with me and somebody, any-body, begins to talk about awful things that we frankly don't need to dwell on, I walk up to them gently shaking my head, No. I place my hand over his or her mouth. Works every time! I say, "Please talk positive around my children." Then we walk away. The boys find this funny. They are almost grown men now, but I still interrupt when some brainless twit starts off on his horror story. I say, "Please don't talk about diabetes horror stories around us. We know more about diabetes than you can imagine. All you are doing is scaring us. You need to help adults to be positive around young people."

Spike and Bo are teen mentors for a wonderful playgroup, Kids With Diabetes, Inc. As teens they have had to learn to stop adults from telling horror stories in front of the kids in the playgroup. Bo is great—he just steps forward, interrupts, and says, "We don't talk like that around the kids."

Do all kids and their families a favor. Educate your family and friends. Take a hint from Dr. Laura: Don't allow people to gos-sip in front of your kids. I find it very upsetting when people launch into their horror stories, and I am not shy about asking them to stop. I must add that I usually go on to explain that the treatment for diabetes has drastically changed. We have blood tests now that allow us pretty good control of blood sugar. Kids can expect long and healthy lives.

You have got to be proactive about this or the scary stuff will float around in your brain and make you miserable. **We like to focus on what can go right with diabetes.** If any child with dia-betes or his family wants to know about what can go wrong, they can ask their doctor, read the complications section of any diabetes self-help manual, or go online. The ADA web site, Diabetes.org, is comprehensive.

Tip: Don't let your 7-year-old child read all the scary stuff at the back of books on diabetes or in the complications sections. Help keep your children away from the scary stuff online. As Dr. Chochinov pointed out to me, even if it's valid information, sometimes kids are too young to understand what they find on the Internet.

When Spike went to the hospital at age seven, Rick bought three identical books on diabetes. We all sat down together and read through them. Spike was a good reader and got to the back of his book before we did. He read all about complications, and it scared him. A year later, when we left for the hospital with Bo, Spike grabbed my arm and said. "Mom, whatever you do, don't let Bo read the section in the back of that book."

When Everything Goes Wrong, How to Get it All Back Together

I have attempted to put things in this book that parents can identify with. Sometimes when you have one or more children with diabetes you can feel overwhelmed. When that happens around here, I try to remind myself that it's the boys who have to live with diabetes. My job is to help them. When really traumatic things happen, I stop and tell myself: "You can do this. This will pass; you have to help the boys get through it."

A wild series of events occurred here last spring. I am sharing this story with you because I think it illustrates a lot of the hands-on care needed when kids get hurt. It starts out scary, but everybody is okay. Spike and Bo recovered completely! This is my e-mail about "the wreck," to my sister, Gebo.

Subj: The Wreck
Date: 3/5/99 - Wednesday

Considering the way things started out, this truly has turned out to be the Happiest Day of My Life. The good news is Bo is in one piece. He has pretty bad whiplash, sore lower teeth, and a cut up mouth. The hair on his hands and legs was singed off. He'll probably have some sore places tomorrow. No cuts, broken bones, or permanent damage.

Typical morning here, got up at 6 AM with Baby Dog and fixed her a gourmet breakfast. Then we woke up Bo and fixed bacon and eggs for him. He grabbed his homework and headed out the door.

This morning there was the usual roar when he turned onto highway 150. Ah, he's safely off to school I thought, lingering by the kitchen window. Then in the blink of an eye, the power went out. Minutes later Bo's friend Blake roared up in his truck and started pounding on the kitchen window. I looked up. "Bodie's been in a car accident." "Is it bad?" "It's pretty bad."

Instantly I was driving fast down our driveway onto highway 150, but there were a hundred stalled cars in my way, so I went the wrong way weaving in and out of cars until I came to the burning telephone pole and saw Bo's Bronco engulfed in a wall of flames. Not good.

I jumped out of my car and started running towards the Bronco. Then the fire chief, Bob Roper, tackled me. I don't know what he was saying cuz maybe I was screaming a little bit. What he was doing was keeping me from running smack dab into a downed power line. Pretty soon I heard him and he was saying, "Bo's not in the car. He's over there." So I ran over to Bo and knelt beside him. There might have been a tear or two, a couple of choking gulps, and then I just ran my hand once over my face and put on that "let's handle this emergency" face, and started checking him out. A hundred people were already there. Somebody handed me a Gatorade to keep Bo's sugars up. A jogger had her hands locked under his neck holding it absolutely still.

Bo never lost consciousness, kept his cool, said he was doing okay. "How could he be?" I thought, listening to the car explode. There were so many friends standing around that Bo only heard the final explosion, didn't see the tower of flames go up when the engine blew, didn't see first the back tire, then the right front tire, ignite and blow. In fact, he asked me if I thought his new stereo would be okay. "Could be." I said. I kept looking at his face—not a scratch on it, just a bloody mouth, his singed arms, his pale hands.

Minutes later the paramedics arrived, and they were good, calm, careful. They went over every inch of Bo's body, put on a neck brace, checked his vital signs, then the team lifted him onto a backboard. About then Rick hobbled up.

He had been in the shower when I yelled, "Bo's been in an accident." His truck was stopped by the traffic jam. Seeing smoke, he bailed out and started running. When he came around the bend to the wall of flames, his Achilles tendon snapped. (Bo will fully recover from whiplash in a few weeks. Rick requires surgery next week and a six-month convalescence.)

Bo said he never saw the other car. He just felt a firm tap and immediately his truck was careening down the roadway, first sideways, then spinning, then trees flew by, then bam! He looked around and saw flames lapping under the dashboard, then reached down to unsnap his safety belt and was surprised when he fell out of his seat onto the passenger door. He didn't know his car was on its side. He unlocked the passenger door and tried to get out. It wouldn't budge. He pushed on it again. It wasn't gonna open. "Okay, I'll try the other door," he thought.

He climbed up to the driver's side, unlocked the door, flames burned the hair off his hands, it wouldn't budge. He jammed his elbow into the door: nothing. He looked around. "I've got a lift-gate," he thought, but gate wouldn't open. That's when the hair on his legs got singed. Flames were lapping up on all sides of his truck now, and he was starting to get scared, so he yelled, "Would somebody help me, open the spare tire latch!" Then he put his shoulder into the back door with all his might, but it wouldn't budge. Now he was feeling a little panicky and started really yelling, "Help, somebody help me!" Nobody moved. "Okay," he thought to himself, looking around, "How are you gonna get out of this thing?" Throwing his shoulder into the glass, flames everywhere, he looked up and noticed the long rectangular piece of glass on the driver's side was gone. He could see the sky. Everything was in slow motion now. Carefully placing his hands on the shattered glass, he climbed up into the arms of a guy who yanked him out. Bo stumbled about twenty feet, until he noticed his neck hurt real bad, so he lay down on the shoulder of the road.

While I was riding in the ambulance with Bo, Rick returned home to gather together our back-up insulin Kit and Cooler. Bo's had burned up in his car.

Earlier, lying on the side of the road, in the gravel, then strapped on the backboard, and later in the ambulance, Bo kept saying how bad he hurt, right at the base of his neck. Once in the hospital, they got him on a gurney, cut off his shirt and started going over him. He kept complaining about this one place on his neck. Couldn't they take off the neck cuff, it was killing him? No. Must be immobile. His sugar was good, 279, blood pressure normal, everything great. Then, off to X ray. This tiny little X-ray tech, about 15 years old, wheeled him in. A few minutes later she came flying out, "Doctor, you better come quick, look at this.

Something is in there, in his neck. It looks like a tumor." Without missing a beat, the ER doctor says, "No, it looks like a rock." She loosened the neck cuff, reached in, and pulled out a great big rock. So much for listening to Bo.

After a couple of hours, we were out of the emergency room and off to the dentist's office for X rays. Somehow, in the course of the accident, Bo's bottom teeth were pushed back. His tongue was pretty chewed up, and his mouth was all bloody. By the time we got to the dentist, his teeth had migrated back. During the chaos, I called Uncle Marty, doctor extraordinaire to report in. Marty said, "Go see an orthopedic surgeon stat." So, it was off to the specialist. By 5:00 PM Bo's X rays had been gone over. The specialist said the pictures looked great! Real clean! He expected no further problems. He put a neck collar on Bo and prescribed anti-muscle spasm medication, codeine for pain and Motrin for inflammation.

On the way home, Bo wanted to stop by the site of his accident. "Geeze, it really burned huh? Damn, I had ten essays in my binder; my English teacher is gonna kill me." Believe it or not, under a piece of melted tire, I found his binder. Not exactly intact, about ¾ of it remained, the cover was melted, it was soaking wet, but the essays were in there. (He turned it in the following Monday.)

Back at home, I put Bo on the couch. Right now Baby Dog is sleeping on Bo's lap, Rick's gone to bed, and I am very very happy. Virginia

My Next E-mail
Subj: You Are Not Going to Believe This, But

That same evening Spike called from Stanford to say he thought he had broken his arm. Friday morning Spike again called to tell us the good news. The good news was that his broken arm was already in a cast. The bad news was that he was going in for surgery the next morning. That changed things around here because I was needed here to help Bo, needed here to help Rick with his surgery, needed here for Baby Dog, and needed at Stanford to be with Spike during his surgery. So, Rick postponed his Achilles tendon surgery, Baby Dog volunteered to watch Bo because Rick was on more pain medication than Bo, and I went to Stanford.

Spike's surgery was supposed to take one hour, but it took four and a half. He now has a metal plate and screws in his elbow. His hospital stay was extended from four hours to two and a half days. On Monday we postponed Spike's final exams and I brought him home. v

Thank heavens, I had Baby Dog, my five-pound Maltese, to help me with all the boys. Besides trying to regulate everybody's insulin, drugs, and bandages, and keeping a sense of humor, there were a number of clerical things to do for the boys. Spike was a freshman at Stanford at the time of his skateboard accident and elbow surgery. Because of the narcotic painkiller he was on for ten days, Spike couldn't stay at school. The drugs caused him to sleep a lot, and he could not manage his diabetes. That's why I brought him home after his surgery. Once at home, I helped Spike locate his teachers by e-mail. Once informed of the accident, his surgery, and the need to be away from school for two weeks, all of his professors cooperated with Spike as far as making up exams or final papers.

I could tell Spike was not happy about leaving campus. But things happen. I gave him no choice. I didn't dwell on it. I just said, "You need to come home and get some help. When you are off pain medication, you can go back to school." In reality, Bo's wreck and Spike's surgery had been so traumatic, it was good for the boys to be together.

Bo had a long recuperation ahead of him and a lot of pain. Everyone in our small town knew about the wreck, but I made a point of letting all his teachers know that Bo would return to school as soon he could. Once again everyone cooperated. Team work.

The kids both felt bad because they felt they had messed up. As I told Bo, "Accidents happen. Of course you didn't do this on purpose. We will get through this. I love you and I am here to take care of you." **When bad things happen, kids need reassurance.**

Allaying Your Secret Fears

We all have them. We don't mention them. Let's get them out in the open and over with. My most terrible fear, the one I never told anybody, from day one was: What about their eyes? I was afraid Spike and Bo would go blind. (According to our endocrinologist, children who get diabetes before puberty don't have eye complications.) Here is how I got over this fear. I was really worried about this blindness thing, never mentioned it, but it was driving me crazy. After about four years, we found our current endocrinologist, Dr. Diana Schwarzbein. This woman changed our lives. After she examined both boys, the four of us were sitting in her office. She is this beautiful woman, young and very smart, and she just looked at my boys with this wonderful expression on her face and said, "Guys, I have never examined two healthier people in my life. You can forget about me telling you how to handle your diabetes. Why don't you tell me how you two guys do it?" That started a beautiful relationship. The boys, relaxed and proud of themselves, began to share everything with Dr. Diana. When they were done talking and she had made

insulin adjustment suggestions and tweaked their diet a little, she asked them to forego French fries and promise never to smoke cigarettes. Then she saw me privately for a few minutes. I'll never forget that first meeting. Dr. Schwarzbein said, "What's wrong, mom? Your kids are in great shape, and yet you seem so upset. What are you scared of?"

"Their eyes," was all I could manage to say. "I'm afraid they'll go blind." "Kids don't have eye complications before puberty," she said. "You'll want to get a pre-puberty baseline vision check just like you did for your other kids. That's it." Regarding growing, Dr. Schwarzbein said kids under good control grow normally. When first diagnosed, a kid might miss out on a growing spurt. With good control, he will catch up. Dr. Schwarzbein went on to explain to me some wonderful things. She told me about how resilient the body is. She said if we begin to see a problem, we'll fix it, that under tight control, gained through frequent blood tests, the body rejuvenates itself. This was good news for me. It allowed me to relax and to quit worrying.

Dating

Kids with diabetes date. Part of the payoff for letting everybody you know understand that your child has diabetes is that the knowledge will become part of the social fabric in your community. Diabetes has not interfered with Spike and Bo developing friendships at any period of their lives. In fact, they seem to have deeper, longer lasting friendships than average. Dating is an extension of friendships. Both boys hang out with their guy friends, have many female friends, and date, just like their peers. The other kids don't care about diabetes. They find it interesting, ask questions when they are at our house, and then just go on being kids.

Marriage

Of course young people with diabetes get married. Kids make friends, young people date, young adults fall in love. I have not seen diabetes interfere with any of the above. Part of this is because we have not kept diabetes a secret from the community. The boys are very open about their diabetes, about snacking and taking injections. There is no mystery to it. Managing diabetes is just a part of life.

Having Children

People with diabetes are at a slightly increased risk of having a child with diabetes. There is no diabetes in our family background; it just popped up with Spike and Bo. Diabetes seems to skip generations. Current research is very near a diabetes vaccine. We don't worry about the future decision to have children, and we can all live with the small risk factor. What about daughters? It's more complicated for a woman with diabetes during pregnancy, but many doctors have experience with diabetic patients. In addition to an experienced OB-GYN doctor, a pregnant woman with diabetes would benefit from the expertise of a good endocrinologist. She should have excellent blood sugar control before she gets pregnant, as those first months are the most important to the baby's health.

Tip: If something is frightening you, talk to your child's endocrinologist about it. No need to buy trouble. He or she can probably put you at ease.

SIBLINGS

When Spike and Bo got diabetes, it mobilized the entire family. Their sisters got involved, were concerned, compassionate, and good sports about the changes that went on in our household. Involving the other kids in helping their brother or sister who has diabetes will strengthen your family. Even younger siblings can be part of the team. Bo was only five years old when Spike was diagnosed. Bo wanted to help. He learned where the low blood sugar food was, practiced giving injections to an orange, and always called for Mom if Spike wasn't feeling well.

When you come home from the hospital, your other children will be concerned, even scared. Be sure and explain to them that everything is going to be all right. Explain that diabetes is a condition you can manage, that their sibling will be okay. Involve them in helping their sibling. Help all the kids get used to the new routine, meals on time, healthy snacks at bedtime, no junk food, no soft drinks in the house, and other changes. Remind them how glad you are that modern medicine provides ways to check the blood for sugar and insulin.

You will be discussing diabetes often. Kids need to hear the same things over and over again to understand them, so you will be educating your children throughout the years. Let them get excited about diabetes research, inhaled insulin trials, islet cell transplants, and improvements in the insulin pump.

Let Siblings Be Part of the Team

Knowing where all your kids are all the time is important, especially when one or more of your children has diabetes. When the kids were in their teens and starting to drive and spend the night at friends' houses, I explained to them that I needed to know where they all were in case I needed help. If Spike should become ill and need help at the local ER, I would need the other kids to come home and take care of Bo, and vice versa. Or if Bo were having a problem, I would want Spike to come home so I didn't have to worry about him. Having all the kids involved in watching out for each other worked for our family. They were always there for each other and for me, and in a crisis would ask what they could do to help.

Diabetes has had quite an effect on our family. Jenny, the oldest, is the health editor for an online magazine, *Chickclick.com*. Mary, next in line, is attending medical school at USC. Spike is majoring in human biology at Stanford, and Bo is studying biomedical engineering at USC. Good things do come out of adversity!

Our entire family wishes you well. Remember, set high goals and enjoy the journey! You will be proud of your children, all of them.

I asked the boys' sisters, Jenny and Mary, to contribute to this section on siblings. Jenny was 14 years old when Spike

was diagnosed, Mary was 12 years old. The first message is from Mary. The second piece is an article Jenny wrote for *Chickclick.com* on the publication of her brothers' book, *Getting a Grip on Diabetes*.

Mary's Thoughts for Siblings

When your sibling is diagnosed with diabetes, you will become an even more important person in his life. You will be needed to do a few essential things. One is to help your family adjust emotionally. Another is to help make the changes that will occur in your household and family's routine as easy and smooth as possible. Yet another is to learn about how to care for your brother or sister and help keep him healthy.

Learning to make things work will be an emotional experience for the whole family; there's no doubt about it. Your parents will be worried about you, too. You've got to let them know from time to time that you're okay, that you're still smiling and playing and going about your life. That way they don't have to feel like you're being neglected while they focus more of their attention on your brother or sister. You can be a real comfort to your parents. Maybe your mom is the one who is in charge of caring for the day-to-day blood tests and shots. Maybe once in a while she gets a little stressed out. You will be able to tell when these times are. So you be the strong one that day. She needs your reassurance. Tell her things are going to be okay. Tell her she is doing a great job. If it's your brother who has diabetes, tell her he is doing well and point out something that is going right. Parents get overwhelmed, too.

After Spike was diagnosed with diabetes, and even more so after Bo was diagnosed, things started changing in our house. The changes were mostly centered on the way we ate. We simply had different foods in our cupboards and did away with some of the junk. It was so easy. We made a big deal out of the special shelf of foods and drinks that were for Spike and Bo's lows. But the things that were no longer on our shelves were not a big deal at all. I never missed them. In fact, I'm sure I'm a healthier eater today because of the changes we made when we were all kids. Our mom has always been a wonderful cook and loves to do a lot of baking. The solution here was easy, too. The size of baking dishes just got smaller. We used little miniature bread pans and little miniature muffin tins. It was fun. Somehow it made baking treats seem even more special. I've been living on my own for years now, my roommate is not diabetic, and I still bake with the smaller-sized dishes. Everybody loves it when I give them miniature loaves of applesauce bread.

Another very important role of the sibling is that of caregiver and educator. Even if you just watch how your diabetic brother or sister goes through a particular routine from day to day and you know nothing else about diabetes, you will become something of an authority on diabetes. You can share your knowledge with friends and classmates and help educate them about diabetes. It will be especially useful for those who will be spending some time around your sibling. Also, there will probably be times when you will want to be directly involved in doing the diabetes stuff. When Spike first came home from the hospital, we all practiced injecting an orange to get the feel for what it is like to give someone a shot. We learned how to draw the insulin, too. You may have better eyesight than your parents, so they may need your help sometimes to make sure they have drawn up the right amount of insulin.

If you are an older sibling, you will probably be babysitting from time to time. You may then be in charge of checking blood sugars, preparing meals, and giving insulin shots. The first couple of times you may feel more comfortable with mom and dad there. Or even when they are gone, you might want to check the blood sugar and then discuss insulin dosage with mom and dad on the phone before you give the shots. The bottom line is, you can do it. Spike and Bo were always such good sports when Jenny and I were in charge. Of course I was a little nervous at first, and they must have known it. Whenever I would give them their shots, they would reassure me and tell me I did a great job. It always made me feel so proud and so touched that they could be worried about how I was feeling when there I was sticking them with needles.

Speaking of needles, no one likes the idea of sticking her little brother with a needle. One thing that helped me feel better about it was accidentally sticking myself once. I hardly felt the needle and there it was sticking right out of my hand. I don't necessarily recommend doing this intentionally, but take a look at the needles used to inject insulin. They are pretty small. As far as blood checks go, go ahead and test your own blood sugar a couple of times when you feel comfortable with it. Then you will know what it feels like. Or, better yet, let your brother prick your finger. He'll probably like getting to do it to you instead of you doing it to him.

Helping take good care of your brother or sister will be one of the best things you can ever do. Your brother or sister will trust you forever. This is your chance to make a real difference in a child's life.

Jenny's Story: Blood, Sugar, Needles

I learned all about needles at age 14. I knew where to find clean ones, how to get rid of dirty ones, and dreamed about the 5-gallon water bottle under the kitchen counter that was filled with used ones. The needles weren't for me—they were for my little brothers.

My little brother Spike was diagnosed with insulin-dependent diabetes on Thanksgiving Day in 1987. He was 7 years old. Bo, my baby brother, was diagnosed exactly one year later. He was just 6 years old. Every day since, they've injected themselves with insulin, tested drops of blood to read their blood sugar and on occasion, they've gone to the emergency room or injected glucagon.

As your Body+Soul editor, I'd like to tell you a little bit about my brothers, the way they handle diabetes, and the book they started writing before they even got home from the hospital so many years ago. And it's not just because I'm proud of them—teen diabetes is on the rise, and what you don't know about diabetes could change your life.

The Boys

My family was determined not to let diabetes get in the way of the boys' enjoying their lives. My mom, dad, sister, and I all learned how to give them shots and do blood tests. The boys began to carry Playmate coolers, filled with food for the day and emergency-sugar stashes for when they had dangerously low blood sugar levels. Every friend, teacher, and neighbor knew about their diabetes and what to do if they needed help.

Since the day they were diagnosed, Spike and Bo have written notes to themselves and each other about how to handle their diabetes. They not only jotted down the basics on what to do in an emergency, they recorded how much they had to eat to go surfing, how often they need Gatorade during a soccer game, and how much insulin they should take when traveling. Basically, they kept track of what they had to do to manage their diabetes while they lived their lives the way they wanted to.

A few years ago, the boys compiled their tips and handed them out to family and friends and to recently diagnosed kids they met. After Spike converted the stapled Tips into a senior project at high school, Bo contributed the technical stuff and built a web site filled with helpful tips for kids, Kidsanddiabetes.com.

My baby brothers (Spike is a junior at Stanford, and Bo's a freshman at USC) are the authors of a new book called *Getting a Grip on Diabetes*. Published by the ADA, it's the first book by diabetic kids for diabetic kids.

Diabetes

Medical studies across the country show diabetes is on the rise. More than 16 million people have diabetes in the United States and about 800,000 more are diagnosed each year. Some (like my brothers) have type 1 diabetes, or insulin-dependent diabetes. But most of them have type 2 diabetes, also called adult-onset diabetes or diet-controlled diabetes.

As the name suggests, type 2 usually strikes adults and is often the result of years of unhealthy eating habits—medical journals often connect it directly to obesity. Type 1 usually strikes kids and teens—my friend Elka was diagnosed when she was 16, and my brothers are helping the family of an 18-month-old girl learn to manage her diabetes.

Diabetes Care journal reports that in the last 10 years alone, the cases of diabetes in the U.S. have increased by one third—from 13 million in 1990 to more than 16 million in 2000. The biggest increase was seen among people 30 to 39 years old (70 percent). But it's not just adults. Studies show that more and more kids and teenagers are being diagnosed with type 2 diabetes, a disease that until recently was seen in people over the age of 40. Bo says, "The number of people, including teens, being diagnosed with diabetes in this country is growing dramatically."

The tendency to develop type 2 diabetes, according to the ADA, can be hereditary, but it usually takes another factor, like unhealthy eating habits or severe weight gain, to trigger the disease. Bo points out that studies show teens often get type 2 diabetes from lack of exercise and eating poorly—high-carb, high-sugar diets. Bo adds, "Basically, kids that eat a lot of fast food and processed foods and sit around all day are at risk for type 2."

The Book—a Message for Both Types

Bo says that *Getting a Grip* is definitely geared toward type 1 diabetes. "But any diabetic can benefit from the book." *Getting a Grip* details things like daily nutrition, exercise, and controlling your sugars and insulin intake. It has sections dedicated to elementary school, participating in sports and outdoor activities, eating out, driving, and even partying. There are also comments from doctors in almost every section that explain the biology behind what Spike and Bo suggest.

"*Getting a Grip* also includes anecdotes about our lives and how we've dealt with diabetes, the day-to-day stuff that comes up when you're living with diabetes," Spike says. "In the book, Bo and I focus on a few important things. First, as a diabetic you can do anything—once you learn how to manage diabetes, it really won't stop you from doing anything.

"Second, don't be afraid to tell people you have diabetes. In fact, you should tell everybody that you're diabetic and talk to them about how to deal if you have low blood sugar. *Getting a Grip* comes with special instructions for friends and teachers."

"Third," and Spike says this is his big thing, "You always have to be a little more careful and a little smarter than your friends. If you are, you can do anything that they can do."

Spike gives the example of surfing: Before he paddles out, he has some food and sticks a tube of frosting in his trunks or wet suit (the high-sugar frosting is for low blood-sugar levels). It takes him two minutes longer to get out in the water but once he's out there, he's tearing it up alongside his friends.

"*Getting a Grip* is written for teens, kids, and their families—and we keep it real upbeat." Spike says. "Our take is that diabetes doesn't have to be scary."

15

Tips for Mom and Dad

Cooler: Keep a packed cooler by the front door, in the car and at school. (You pack it.)

Low blood sugar: Carry cake frosting in your purse, briefcase, athletic bag, and in the car.

Symptoms: Give a copy to all friends, teachers, coaches, friends' parents, etc. Tape a copy of Symptoms inside the top of each cooler. See page 174.

Granola bars: Always carry a granola bar.

Sports tournaments: Don't forget that after exercising, warm muscles absorb glucose for several hours. You require less insulin following heavy exercise.

What About Halloween?

First we talked about it, the whole family together. All of your kids can follow these basic guidelines. The fun part about Halloween is gathering up all the candy, sorting the candy, and telling your friends about your giant candy haul. So tell your child:

▍ Yes, you get to go trick-or-treating.
▍ Yes, you can gather up as much candy as you like.

- Yes, you can sort your candy.
- Yes, you can eat a piece or two that night.
- You can even keep the candy you really like and use it when you have low blood sugars. (If this works for you, put the bite-sized candy in a special drawer in the kitchen.)

On Halloween we had dinner early, around 4 o'clock. (You may need to lower the short-acting insulin dose if your child is wildly excited. There will be lots of Halloweens, you will figure this out on the first one.)

Here are some tips for trick-or-treating.

- Mom or Dad, carry your child's blood testing kit.
- Mom or Dad, carry lots of protein snacks. Have a packed cooler in the car.
- You will be with your child while they're trick-or-treating, so every half hour or so hand him a piece of string cheese or jerky.
- When you get home, he can sort the candy. Take the candy he doesn't like off his hands. (Toss it or give it away. Don't keep it around the house.)
- Trade good sugarless stuff for the candy they can part with. (To help eliminate candy from the house, I had a bag of sugarless gum and small items my boys liked, such as GI Joe men, for trading. We made such a big deal out of trading that for years what my boys talked about and looked forward to was the after trick-or-treat trading.)

Spike and Bo were fortunate to have helpful big sisters. They sold piles of their candy to their sisters. (I had arranged this deal with their sisters before we went trick-or-treating, funding the girls with a handful of dimes and quarters.) Finally, you will be left with a small pile of their favorite candies. "Great!" you say.

"Good job. You have collected candy we can use when you have low blood sugars."

My boys could resist candy. Some kids cannot. If your child isn't very interested in sweets, he can keep a small bag of candy for a couple of days. If he can't resist candy, then you need to store some of his candy stash to bring out when he has low blood sugars.

For a day or two after Halloween, I sent one small piece of candy in their lunch, like a miniature Tootsie Roll. They loved breaking the rules if only for a day or two.

Their big sisters cooperated by trading their sugarless gum for the boys' candy, by buying the boys' candy, and by keeping their own candy stashes completely out of sight. I also asked the girls to be done with their Halloween candy in two or three days. Jenny and Mary took their Halloween candy to school and with their teachers' permission, handed it out in class.

The Halloween party. There is a second way to handle Halloween. You can have a Halloween party at your house and completely avoid the candy issue. Here are some fun things to do at a candy-free Halloween party. This works for very little kids, as they get older they are going to want to go trick-or-treating with their friends. (That's okay, you just go too!)

- Wear costumes.
- For little kids, have a costume parade around the yard or around the living room. Everyone wins a prize. Prizes can be sunglasses, squirt guns, GI Joes, little dolls, bracelets, tiaras, balls, sugarless candy, sugarless gum.
- Bob for apples.
- Toss bean bags.
- Decorate brown bags to take your goodies home in.

- Pin the tail on the donkey (For kids under four, you don't even need to use a blindfold, they still miss the tail).
- Have good snacks sitting out: string cheese, crackers and peanut butter, sliced summer sausage, veggies and kid dip (yogurt).
- Serve dinner.

What About the Pump?

An account of two teens who have had great success with the pump can be found in Spike and Bo's book, *Getting a Grip on Diabetes*. Their chapter on the pump also includes an in-depth discussion by Dr. Marc Weigensberg, pediatric endocrinologist. Children, even very young ones, with good support from their parents and health care team can wear a pump successfully, and many of them get better blood sugar control with fewer lows. If you think you are interested in using the insulin pump, talk with your doctor or diabetes educator. If your child is still thriving on insulin injections like Spike and Bo, it is nice to know that down the line, the insulin pump is an option.

Carbohydrate Counting

Virtually everyone who takes 3 or more insulin injections a day (or uses an insulin pump) counts carbs. Carbohydrate in food is what raises blood sugar. Carbohydrate is found in cereals, pasta, and starchy vegetables. Most people don't know that it is also found in fruit, milk, and sugary foods. All sources of carbohydrate raise your blood sugar about the same—a brownie and a baked potato have about the same effect on blood sugar. (It's when you start looking for vitamins that the potato pulls ahead as healthier to eat.)

You'll need good records for a week or two to see how much insulin you need to "cover" 15 grams of carbohydrate. On your records, you'll note the number of carbs in each meal, your insulin dose, amount and time of exercise, and your blood sugar numbers before and two hours after taking the first bite of the meal. Then you and your doctor or educator can look at your records and decide what your insulin to carbohydrate ratio is. Taking one unit of Humalog for each 15 grams of carb is the standard, but each person is different according to his/her insulin sensitivity. You and your doctor will figure out how many units of insulin cover 15 grams of carb for you. You'll also figure out how much insulin to take to bring down blood sugar that is 50 mg/dl above your target range. For more information about carb counting, ask your diabetes educator or dietitian. You'll find that measuring the serving size really helps. Check the serving size on the food label. Are you having two or three servings of cereal in your bowl? Then you are also having two or three times as much carbohydrate as is listed on the food label! You can learn more from the ADA *Complete Guide to Carb Counting*, published in 2001.

Kitchen Tricks and Techniques

Here are some things I did when Spike and Bo were little, so they wouldn't feel like they were missing out on anything, including Mom's baking.

First, I bought a $2 set of teeny tiny juice glasses—you know, the kind with bright oranges painted on them. They hold 4 ounces tops. When Spike or Bo just had to have a glass of orange juice (carbohydrate), they got a whole glass, but it was such a small glass, it was okay.

I bought small dessert bowls. For years when they just had to have ice cream, I'd serve them a small scoop that filled the little bowl. I bought miniature loaf pans for baking and tiny muffin tins. When the boys had a miniature dessert, there weren't many carbohydrates involved. If we made homemade doughnuts, we made doughnut holes and sugared them with Equal. I bought smaller plates to use for dinner. That way everyone could have a plate full of food, but the servings of carbs would be smaller. This went for the entire family.

My kids like waffles. Waffles are fun because little kids can pick them up in their hands. I used Bisquick mix. Now, waffles are just a bunch of carbohydrates, so here's how I always make them. Put some Bisquick in a bowl. Add an egg. Add a tablespoon of oil. Add half the normal amount of whole milk. Add two or three huge spoonfuls of cottage cheese to the batter. Mix the batter lightly. They cook up great. The cottage cheese is protein. By adding cottage cheese, you have just doubled the batter, so the carb count of a waffle is cut in half.

My kids hated sugar-free syrup, so I would buy one bottle of sugar free and one bottle of low-sugar syrup and mix them. We used very little syrup, but now the amount of sugar in the low-sugar syrup was reduced by half.

When Spike went off to college, we went up to Stanford for parents weekend where we had breakfast at Spike's fraternity house. As we were going through the food line, Spike said, "Mom, I want you to see something." At that he held up a giant 12-ounce glass of orange juice. "I don't know what you were thinking when we were little but, *this* is a glass of orange juice!"

16

How to Start A Playgroup

The playgroup acts as a support group. We discovered that by getting together once a month for the kids, we were also helping the emotional needs of the parents. Parents of very young kids are inspired by active, happy, can-do teens. Generally what happens at a playgroup is—the kids play. The playgroup parents might have crafts set up at a table for the really young children. They bring balls, Frisbees, and games to the park for the older kids. The teens find themselves acting as mentors for the youngsters, encouraging parents and helping out. During the time the families spend together each month, a lot of information is shared. Kids look forward to coming to play, teens look forward to being peer models, and parents have a place to ask questions and share valuable experience. Nothing beats asking another parent how they did it.

Our local playgroup was started mainly through the efforts of Patty Conlan. This is what Patty says about getting started.

If You Build It, They Will Come.

■ Pick a day, time, and a place to meet each month. We meet at a local park.

- Invite other families. At our first playgroup, there were only two.
- How to find others:
    > Place a notice in the calendar section of the local newspaper: Support Group for Kids With Diabetes, Saturday 10:00 AM to noon at: (name location)
    > Send flyers to doctors and hospitals.
    > Inform all the schools in your area that a playgroup exists.
    > Distribute flyers at different venues, such as local pharmacies, the ADA walk, the JDF walk, your local county fair, your library.
- Make your phone number available.

As the playgroup grew, the work was divided up. One family spread the word, another brought games, another provided healthy snacks, and yet another family put together helpful literature to hand out. As the group evolved, we kept reminding each other that our playgroup would be positive, positive, positive.

Getting Involved in a Playgroup

Some of us are organizers, while some of us just want to attend an occasional monthly playgroup. That's okay. An effective playgroup is a place where kids and families can just go for fun, support, and encouragement. Other families might want to get more involved like Jeff and Diane Valine, whose 3-year-old daughter Laura is a member of our local playgroup. The web site they volunteered to start, Kidswithdiabetes.org, has helped reach out to families all across the country.

New Kid Program

The playgroup also started a New Kid program. The original families independently found themselves going to the homes of newly diagnosed kids. We would give them a copy of the boys' book: *Getting a Grip on Diabetes*, a copy of *Taking Diabetes to School,* and a Playmate cooler packed with everything needed to treat low blood sugar. Playgroup parents have added teddy bears, backpacks, glucose monitors, and back-to-school information to the New Kid Kits.

Hosting Special-Event Parties

The first special event hosted by the playgroup was a Halloween party. The Halloween party was held in the park. Kids wore costumes, and we held a costume parade for the little kids. The teens judged the parade. Everyone won a prize. Some of the families made little booths; there was gold fishing, apple bobbing, bean-

bag toss, face painting, and even a giant jumping room. We made 20 fabric capes for kids who didn't come in costume and bought $2 tiaras for the little girls.

The menu. There was a piñata filled with sugarless candy, protein bars, Night Bites, tubes of frosting, and little trinkets. We had a popcorn machine and coolers full of diet sodas, fruit juice, and bottled water. For the main course, there were platters of deli meats, rolls, vegetables, dip, and fruit. Throughout the party, moms and dads would sit down on the grass with their kids, do a quick blood test to check their child's blood sugar, and then carry on!

Thirty-five kids showed up for that first Halloween party and they loved it!

Getting Funded

In the beginning, our local playgroup was parent funded. By the time the size of the playgroup had grown to fifty kids, it was time to do something about money. Other groups may not need to get this organized. Perhaps you are from a very small town and your group is four or five kids. We decided to become a non-profit organization.

In order to raise funds, write grants, and ask for big sums of money (tax deductible), it was necessary to achieve a nonprofit status. Patty started the ball rolling by obtaining the documents. I helped her fill out the paperwork. The most active parents were asked to sit on the board of directors, as well as a teenager.

To form a nonprofit organization:

▪ Call your State Board of Equalization Office
▪ Ask for the 1099 Form

■ You will need to meet certain requirements. We found that we needed to:
  • Form a Board of Directors
  • Choose a President
  • Choose a Treasurer
  • Choose a Secretary
  • Conduct regular Board of Directors Meetings

Writing Grants

Once the nonprofit paperwork came through, we began to solicit donations from local groups and write grants. Each grant funding organization required our 1099 Form, a year-end budget, and a detailed grant application. We found that grant writing only works when a parent who likes to do this tedious work volunteers to do it because she/he wants to. We have been fairly successful in obtaining funds. No one in Kids With Diabetes, Inc. is paid. The supplies we purchase with grant money and donations are:

■ Craft items for the monthly playgroup
■ Snacks for the monthly playgroup
■ Books, manuals, teddy bears, coolers, and the supplies to fill the coolers, etc., which are given out to new kids.

Getting Teens Involved

At our playgroup, our teens just naturally evolved into mentors for the younger kids. As time went on, Spike left for college and Bo realized he, too, would be leaving the group. We decided to develop a teen mentor program to help prepare the younger teens to become spokespersons for the group. (See page 159.) By now, reporters were calling for interviews, schools were calling for speakers, and politicians were asking how they could help. Bo, Vanessa, Kelly, and Bridget (kids from the group) began handling the school talks. We always sent a kid to talk to reporters and politicians. After all, this is about kids, and they are the ones living with diabetes.

We held training seminars for our younger teens to help prepare them to talk to new kids and parents, give interviews to the press, meet politicians, and give school presentations. The school presentations ranged from the kind eight-year-old Brian Jeffery gave to his third-grade class, to an elaborate presentation made by Bridget Conlan (age 10) to her fifth grade class, to Vanessa and Bo's in-service workshop for school nurses, to full-blown school assemblies. Whatever the kids and teens want to do, you can help set it up.

Tip: Help parents in your group to let the kids answer questions. This is empowering to kids, and you will be floored by how adults react when it's the kids who do the talking!

Planning for Playgroups

Once your playgroup grows to over 20 kids or so, you may need to do a little more formal planning each month. Here is Patty Conlan's planning outline.

Two Weeks Prior to Playday

- Print and send out notices (currently 80 names)
- Fax notices to local newspapers

Day Before Playday

▐ Reminder telephone calls to families

▐ Pick up donated refreshments from local businesses

Playday

▐ Reserve park tables by 7:00 AM

▐ Arrive 15 minutes early to set up chairs, refreshments, games, activities, or crafts

▐ Items to bring: literature, large and small coolers, boy and girl tote bags (stocked)

▐ Stay 15 minutes late for clean up and break down

▐ In case of rain, have an alternate indoor site in mind and make the arrangements

Other

▐ Arrange for interesting guest speakers (MiniMed pump sales rep, successful college student, surfer, glucose monitor rep)

▐ Coordinate theme parties throughout the year: Spring Fling, Summer Fun, Halloween, Holiday Party, and Easter Egg Hunt

THE TEEN MENTOR PROGRAM

The teens in our playgroup, Kids With Diabetes, became very active forming a Teen Mentoring program. Here are some ideas that may help you guide your teens. Some of our kids are natural speakers; some needed a little practice. Getting the teens together once or twice a year to help each other with their presentations turned out to be a wonderful experience. The first Teen Mentor Seminar was held at our ranch. This is an overview of what the teens talked about and the agenda for one of their meetings.

The Teen Mentor: What You Can Do to Help!

■ Go to the playgroup and interact with the younger kids. By being there, you are acting as a role model.

■ Answer the kids' questions.

■ Talk with new parents. When new parents see happy, healthy, athletic teens, it inspires confidence and hope. By seeing you and talking with you, the parents will relax a little about dealing with diabetes, and it will help their young kids.

■ Deliver coolers, manuals, bears, etc., to kids. New kids love to get these things.

■ By meeting you, other kids find out that they are not alone.

■ When you give a new kid a cooler, he will be safe when away from home.

■ When you give out a manual written by kids in your playgroup, you help kids to get organized and see how they can do everything they want.

■ You can give talks to school kids.

■ You can e-mail kids who contact Kidswithdiabetes.org.

■ You can be available to talk to reporters.

TEEN MENTOR SEMINAR
AGENDA

Introduce each other.

Bo   Teens' role in the playgroup

           Mentors, role models, offer hope and inspiration

           Teens' role as a spokesperson for kids with diabetes

           Talk about speaking to groups of kids

                 Typical questions grade schoolers ask

                 Loaded questions

                 Guidelines for talking to classrooms

	Talking to parents, reassure them, be positive, don't give insulin advice
Group	Individuals practice speaking to groups
Vanessa	The Pump Option
Kelly	Basic pump info
	Putting their pump stories on the web page
	Web page reaching out: e-mailing other kids
Joanna	Advocacy
Bo	Teens invited to put items on the web page
	How to: write it up, get a picture
Group	Teen concerns
Deirdre	Plan the Spring Fling
	Ideas, handouts, sign up, invite other teens to help
Bo	Remember to be positive, positive, positive
Group	Prepare "New Kid" kits and coolers
Lunch	Teens practice making lunch: prepare stir-fry

When you get together with your teens in preparation for speaking to groups of school kids, it helps if your teen speaker has an idea of what kinds of questions the kids might ask. In our group, our teens practiced answering these questions until they were comfortable.

In preparation for speaking to an assembly of fourth, fifth, and sixth graders, Bo prepared the following guide for our Teen Mentors.

Answering Questions that Grade School Kids Frequently Ask

Here are some questions that kids have asked and my answers. Your answers may be different from mine. Sometimes there are loaded questions, questions that you find personal, or that you may be uncomfortable answering. When this happens, you do not need to answer the question. Or you can say, "That's a little personal. I am here to talk about diabetes in general."

Little kids are a lot smarter than you might think, and sometimes they ask you questions to which you don't know the answers. Don't be afraid to say, "I don't know." At my last talk, a kid asked me how insulin is made. When I was answering the question, I realized I only had a general idea of the process. So I gave the kid a general answer and then said, "I don't know exactly how the process works. But, I'll write to Eli Lilly and ask them for the answer." The kids loved it!

Before you go to speak to a group, ask the teacher for a list of questions from the students. This way you will get an idea of what they know and what they are interested in. When I speak to groups, I give them some background and then launch into the student written question list. By using their questions, I am prepared with my answers, and it immediately involves the students.

Sometimes kids want to know what they can do to help. First of all, they are helping by being there and learning about diabetes. Encourage them to help their friends who have diabetes and to know who their congressman is. In our district, it is Congressman Elton Gallegly. If they want to write letters, ask them to write to their congressman and ask him to fund diabetes research.

Props

Kids love to see stuff when you are talking. This is what I take along on talks:

▪ **A copy of:** *Getting a Grip on Diabetes*. You can pass it around, use the book as a reference when you are talking. Just put post-its on the pages you want to refer to.

- **A packed Cooler:** Make sure you have frosting in it.
- **My Kit:** I usually do a finger prick blood test, and let the kids read the results. Then they can figure out whether I need carbohydrate or insulin. The kids are very interested in this process.

The Talk

Give a little background about yourself. Here's mine:

I am a senior at Nordhoff High School where I serve as the ASB Vice President and play varsity soccer. I am enrolled in four AP classes, and I am college bound. My favorite thing to do is surf. I love sports and especially like to snowboard. I enjoy working on my car, and I put a lot of time into a diabetes playgroup.

I have two older sisters, and one older brother who is attending college. My sister Mary is in medical school; my sister Jenny is a writer.

We live on a ranch where we have raised horses, cows, sheep, pigs, chickens, and ducks. Now we have cats, a golden retriever, and Baby Dog.

My future plans are to go college and become involved in the study of biomedical engineering.

About writing a book: My brother and I have both had diabetes since we were six and seven years old. Over the years, we learned how to do everything to care for our diabetes. When you have diabetes, you must balance your food and exercise with your insulin. A couple of years ago, we realized that we have a lot to share with other kids with diabetes, so we sat down and wrote it all down. Our book is laid out logically. It is just all you need to know if you are a kid and you have diabetes. We give kids tips on how to be safe when they are away from home, at school, and while playing sports.

Once we had written the book, we started giving it away. Kids and their parents liked it so much we realized it was very helpful, so we sent a copy to the ADA. They decided to publish our book so it will be available to tens of thousands of kids with diabetes.

We are very happy that our years of experience have been turned into something that will help so many kids and their families. We like to tell kids: **You can do anything with diabetes. You just have to know how!**

Frequently Asked Questions

1. How old were you when you first found out you had diabetes?
Six

2. Type 1 or Type 2?
Type 1, also called insulin-dependent or juvenile-onset diabetes

3. Do you have to do blood tests? How often? Why? How? How does it work?

I generally do a blood check before every meal. On more active days, like when I am going surfing or snowboarding, I'll check even more often. A blood check tells you how much sugar you have in your blood. If you have a lot of sugar in your blood, then you need to take some insulin to distribute that sugar to your cells.

There are many ways to do it. I use two different methods. In both cases, you have to prick your finger or arm and get a drop of blood. It doesn't really hurt because you use a very small lancet. With the first method, you put a drop of blood on a chemically treated strip. You leave the blood there 60 seconds. Then you wipe off the blood and wait another 60 seconds. The strip will change colors. Light colors indicate low blood sugar, and dark colors indicate high blood sugar. The bottle of strips has a scale that helps you find out what your blood sugar is. I like to keep myself between 120 and 180. People without diabetes almost always have a blood sugar of 80.

The second method to measure blood sugar is by using a glucose meter. You get a drop of blood and let the machine absorb it. In 15–30 seconds, the machine gives you a number showing where your blood sugar level is. The good thing about the meter is it is faster, and it keeps track of your numbers for you. The down-side of using the machine is that sometimes it can be inaccurate. Then you have to retest using the visual strips and recalibrate your machine.

4. Do you have to have insulin shots? When? Where? How often? How did you learn to give them?

When I was young I took two shots a day, one in the morning with my breakfast and one at night with my dinner. I used regular insulin and NPH, long-lasting insulin. Now I take

5 shots a day. I take them in the morning before breakfast, at lunch, and before dinner. I take 5 shots because I use regular insulin and Ultralente. You can't mix these two kinds of insulin, so I take each in a separate shot.

When I was 13, I switched from NPH to Ultralente because Ultralente is a longer acting, smoother insulin. There are no peaks, therefore you don't have to eat exactly on schedule and there are fewer lows.

5. Do you miss any foods? Favorite food?

Not really. If somebody is having a piece of pie I eat a tiny slice. Favorite food is an In & Out burger.

6. Did you trick or treat when you were younger?

Of course I did. I just didn't eat too much candy.

7. Why aren't blood tests done on thumbs or pinkies or are they?

Some people use all their fingers including their thumb and pinky. I don't use the thumb because it is ultra sensitive and constantly in use.

8. Can a person outgrow diabetes or is there a cure?

You cannot outgrow type 1 diabetes. There is a cure on the horizon. Most people can control type 2 diabetes by carefully changing their diet and exercising.

9. How often do you have "lows"?

When I was little, I had quite a lot of lows, several a week. It just comes with the territory. Usually I would catch it when I was dropping and drink my Gatorade or eat a candy bar.

10. Does diabetes affect how you exercise? What's your favorite exercise?

I have to check my blood sugar before exercising, adjust my insulin down, and take in more calories, especially carbohydrates.

When surfing, I eat a lot before I go out in the water and only stay out about an hour at a time. Then I come in, grab a snack, and go right back out. I also carry a tube of frosting in my wetsuit sleeve.

If anything, diabetes is an incentive to exercise. Exercise helps keep my blood sugars down. I exercise everyday: I either surf, snowboard, bike ride, ride motorcycles, play soccer, play racquetball, work out, shoot baskets, swim, or play football with my friends. You name it, I do it.

11. Can you ever eat at anybody else's house?

Of course; I eat everything imaginable. But I eat a balanced diet. That means I eat protein at every meal or snack and hardly ever eat any candy. I eat carbohydrates at every meal for energy.

12. Do your meals have to be punctual?

When I was little, I always ate every two hours. Now I eat on the school's schedule, but I have to have breakfast, lunch, and dinner plus snacks.

13. Do you ever get to sleep in?

I always sleep in on the weekends. However, I plan for it. I eat plenty of protein the night before, so I will have sugar/glucose in my system until I want to get up.

14. Do you have other friends or pen pals that have diabetes?

My brother has diabetes, and I am the teen mentor for a playgroup of 50 kids with diabetes.

15. Have you ever been to a diabetic summer camp?

Nope, I was always busy during the summer traveling and having fun with my family. Plus, I live in Upper Ojai, so going to camp would be like going to my backyard.

16. Can you have cake on your birthday?

Yes, a small slice and ice cream too. I just have protein with it.

17. Was it scary when you found out that you had diabetes?

No, because my brother had had diabetes for a year. I had been watching him deal with diabetes. He was my idol anyway, so at six years old I figured that if my brother had diabetes, I might as well have it. It was scary though when my brother was first diagnosed.

18. Was it scary when you had your first shot?

After all the excitement of having to be in the hospital with all the doctors, the blood test hurt more than the shots, so no.

19. Was it scary when you gave yourself your first shot?

This was a little bit nerve racking, but my friends were all there encouraging me to do it. After I gave myself that first shot, it was clear sailing.

20. Do you have a machine that takes your blood test for you?

Yes, it's called a lancet device. It actually pricks your finger for you.

21. How do you feel about having diabetes?

It's just something to deal with. It's just like somebody who has asthma. They have to remember to carry their inhaler with them and use it when they need it.

22. Do you wake up sometimes and wish you didn't have diabetes?

I don't make a point of thinking that. Some good things have come from it. But if I had my choice, I would rather not have diabetes.

23. What symptoms did you have that indicated you had diabetes?

I had the classic symptoms of diabetes: frequent urination, I drank a lot of water, and I had a stomachache and headache due to high blood sugar. None of this escalated to a dangerous level, since my brother already had diabetes and we were on the lookout for it.

24. Has diabetes changed your relationships with friends? Girlfriends?

No, if anything it has actually strengthened my bonds with my friends, because from age six they have always been interested in it. Often in restaurants, I make friends because people ask about my insulin kit. My friends have often helped me when I needed it. With girlfriends, it's been the same way. Once people know me, and they know I have diabetes, they don't even think twice about it.

25. Do you miss being a "normal kid"?

Since I don't miss out on anything that my friends do, I feel just as normal as they are.

26. Is it hard not eating candy? Eating the right foods?

No, because at this point I don't like candy much. However, I always have a candy bar in my car, backpack, or cooler, so if I am feeling low I can eat it. Or, during soccer practice if I need energy, I eat a candy bar.

It's not hard eating the right foods, not when you have a mom who cooks really well. The right kind of food tastes really great. But, when I eat fast foods, I make a conscious effort to eat a lot of protein instead of lots of carbohydrate.

27. Is there a food group you have to eat more of than most people would?

I probably eat more protein than most people.

28. Do people treat you differently because you have diabetes?

Maybe on occasion, I get more attention. If I am seen shooting up, people come over to talk to me because maybe they have an uncle or sister with diabetes, or they have diabetes.

29. Have you ever fainted during a "low"?

Yes, on one occasion, when I was 6. I woke up really early in the morning to go to Catalina with my brother and my mom. All the excitement caused a low blood sugar. They brought me around by putting frosting in my mouth. It took less than a minute for me to wake up.

30. What's the worst part about having diabetes? Any good parts?

When I was younger, probably the worst part was all the responsibility tacked on to having diabetes. My parents helped a lot. I just had to pay attention all the time. Now that I am older and completely take care of it myself, I guess the ups and downs of my blood sugars is the biggest pain in the neck.

31. Do you have to bring your lunch so you can eat right? Do you carry extra stuff in your car or when you are away from home?

When I was little, I did take my own lunches to school. For one thing, my mom made better lunches than the cafeteria did. It was easier for her to pick out what was a balanced diet than for me to have to think about it. Now that I am in high school and have a car, I drive off campus everyday and buy what I want to eat.

I always carry extra food! That's probably the most important thing. Never be away from food.

17

Helpful Info

EXCITING NEW PRODUCTS AND RESEARCH

New Insulin

A new insulin comes out this year, 2001. It will be a true one-time-a-day insulin. Insulin glargine reaches its peak four hours after injection and stays stable for the rest of the day. This will give your specialist one more tool in helping manage your child's blood sugars.

The GlucoWatch Biographer

Spike worked for Cygnus the summer of 2000 and was impressed by the quality of this device. The GlucoWatch is worn like a watch. An arm prick or finger prick is required in the morning to calibrate the watch. Once it warms up, the GlucoWatch provides a blood sugar reading up to every twenty minutes for 12 hours. For nighttime use, another finger prick and calibration are needed. An additional exciting feature of the watch is the alarm. The alarm goes off when blood sugars are very low, very high, or when blood sugars are dropping rapidly.

Cygnus produces the GlucoWatch, which was recently approved by the FDA for use by adults with diabetes. Approval for use by children is expected in the next year or two.

New Meter Pricks Your Arm

The AtLast blood sugar meter came out in 2000 and the FreeStyle meter in early 2001. This is something we wished for when the kids were little. Both Spike and Bo were alerted to the availability of the new meters by 16-year-old Julia Halprin, who contacted Spike via e-mail. Julia said she couldn't even feel the test and liked it much better than the old finger-prick style meters. Spike and Bo agree. Both meters require a smaller amount of blood, are less traumatic than pricking the finger, and give a blood sugar reading in 15 seconds. These meters will make monitoring young children so much easier.

My sons have found communicating with other kids and families about diabetes to be very rewarding. They heard about the new meters because Julia had read their book and wanted to help them. She emailed Spike to thank him for the book, and followed up his return email with a recommendation for the FreeStyle. She said:

I cannot stress what a difference it makes. And while I joke about having tiny constellations on my arms, my hands are feeling so much better. It is true that our insurance did not cover the FreeStyle for the first two to three weeks, but after my dad spent many days badgering the representatives and filing an appeal, Health Net finally agreed to cover it. That's one small victory for the family!

Diabetes Research

Spike and Bo's sister Mary worked in Dr. Fred Levine's Diabetes Research Lab at the medical school at UCSD. We asked Dr. Levine to summarize his research and Mary put it into lay terms.

Beta cells in the pancreas don't work in type 1 diabetes because they have been attacked by the immune system. Beta cells make insulin and help keep blood sugar levels normal. Therefore, one way to treat diabetes would be to replace the lost beta cells. For this to be successful, the new cells have to act like the old ones, but avoid being killed by the immune system. They have to secrete insulin to keep blood sugar levels normal.

We are working with cells that originally came from humans to try and avoid the added problems of rejection by the recipient's immune system. There aren't anywhere near enough human donors to transplant their tissue directly to all of the diabetics in need. So, we are working with cell lines. This means that we have taken primary cells (actual fully developed pancreatic cells from adult pancreas or fetal islets) and tinkered with them, so that they don't die. These cells are effectively immortal. A donor's primary cells only have a limited life span, but the cell lines we work with can continue to divide, allowing us to tinker with them to get them to secrete insulin in response to changing blood sugar levels.

We are now having more success with finding ways to get our cell lines to make more insulin. And not just make it at random, but make more insulin when exposed to more glucose! This is good.

SYMPTOMS

This form is from *Getting a Grip on Diabetes*. This is what works for us. Replace Bo's name with your child's name and list your specific symptoms. Give this to all teachers, coaches, parents, and close friends.

When Bo shows these Symptoms:

Mild	Headache
	Stomachache
Serious	Feels empty
	Shaky hands
	Feels faint
Extreme	Very upset, crying, angry

Do this: Give fruit drink (Gatorade) from backpack
Follow with granola bar, crackers, then jerky
(He should feel better in 3–5 minutes)

- **Your Role:** These symptoms are listed in the order they usually appear. If you are with Bo while he is feeling empty and is shaky, crying, or upset, then you need to open the juice can or Gatorade, put it into his hands, and make sure he drinks it. Hand him the opened granola bar and make sure he eats it.
- **Why?** These symptoms occur because his blood sugar is dangerously low. He is about to pass out. At this point his thinking is cloudy, he cannot function, and he needs sugar!
- **Call:** If you see the more serious symptoms after giving a sugar drink, give more sugar drink. In about 10 minutes, follow with cookies, milk, crackers, chips, and jerky. Then call Virginia (mom) or Rick (dad).

Extreme Emergency:

If Bo should pass out: Open frosting in backpack

Squirt all of it into the corner of his mouth between cheek and gums.

If no frosting is available, put sugar in the corner of his mouth between cheek and gums. A soon as he is alert enough to swallow, follow with a fruit drink, real Coke, or Gatorade. Call Virginia, call Rick. If no luck, call 911 or go to a hospital. Tell them he is suffering from low blood sugar, which is insulin shock, and he needs glucose.

Mom's phone numbers: Home:

Cell: Business:

Dad's phone numbers: Home:

Cell: Business:

Doctor's phone number: Office:

Emergency number:

Hospital phone number:

Note: Have a "Permission to Treat" document on file at your local hospital and at your school.

GLUCAGON INSTRUCTIONS

Glucagon isn't just sugar as the name sounds. It is an anti-insulin hormone. That's why even when you can't eat any food, an injection of glucagon will raise your blood sugar immediately.

When Do You Use Glucagon?

Inject Spike with glucagon if you can't wake him up or if he is so disoriented that he doesn't make sense, and you can't get him to eat. If he throws up once, he should not be left alone. He should call home so they can check on him over the next few hours. If he throws up twice, he should go to the clinic at school. Go with him; he should not go alone. Use the glucagon if he passes out or is too woozy to do anything. Call 911 if things get out of hand.

How Do You Use Glucagon?

1. Inject the liquid in the syringe into the bottle of glucagon powder.
2. Shake the bottle until the glucagon dissolves and becomes clear.
3. Draw all the glucagon solution into the syringe. (For kids under 45 pounds, use ½.)
4. Inject all the solution into the leg or butt.
5. Put Spike on his side, because when he wakes up, he may throw up.
6. Give him food as soon as he wakes up: Gatorade, cookies, crackers, or anything he can eat.

Keep glucagon in your fridge. Always take a glucagon kit with you on trips.

WHAT EVERYONE NEEDS TO KNOW SO THEY CAN HELP

Give this sheet to all teachers, coaches, parents, and close friends. (Substitute your child's name for Bo's.) This is an explanation of why your child sometimes needs extra calories. Once teachers, coaches, and friends have an understanding of what is going on with your child's body they can help.

Maintaining normal blood sugar in a growing kid requires an absolute constant flow of calories into the system. Bo must be allowed to eat the moment he senses his blood sugar is low or dropping, in addition to his scheduled snacks.

- **Food:** He eats when he feels low.

  Must eat every 2 hours.

  Needs more carbohydrate when he exercises and takes exams.
- **Help:** Bo doesn't always feel a low coming on. If you notice odd behavior, ask him if he needs calories.
- **Vomiting:** Requires immediate calories, liquids, and care at home.
- **Injury:** Can make blood sugar soar, then fall. If he is injured, call mom. She will come down and do some tests.
- **Blood checks:** Bo will need to do blood checks at school sometimes. All the kids know about these. Do not send Bo off alone for a blood check. He is probably checking his blood because he is feeling low, and he may need some help to do the test and eat.
- **Call home:** Bo needs to call home when he feels odd or bad. First, have him snack. Then have a student walk to the office with him. Low sugar can cause him to become disoriented.
- **Understanding:** Teachers should not humiliate Bo about his calorie needs.
- **Vigilance:** Bo plays all-star soccer, surfs, and snowboards. He can do anything. We simply must be vigilant EVERY TIME.

RECIPES

I cook the following fast meals in a non-stick, top of the stove, wok-type fry pan.

Breakfast Burrito: This is Spike and Bo's favorite thing to eat for breakfast. After breakfast you can roll one up and pack it for their lunch. Their friends like these breakfast burritos so much that sometimes the boys would take extras to school to share.

Per serving:
2 eggs
½ potato, chopped
green onion, chopped
1 Tbsp butter
1 oz Monterey Jack cheese, a handful, grated
1 slice bacon or sausage
1 tortilla (flour, 6")

1. Cook sausage until done in a separate pan, or micowave bacon until just crisp.
2. Saute the potato in butter. When the potatoes are soft, add the chopped green onion. Reduce to low heat. Toss in eggs and stir. When the eggs are done, sprinkle sausage or bacon on top, then cover with grated cheese.
3. Put flour tortillas, one at a time in the pan for a few seconds, flip. Fill tortilla and serve.

Serve with:
Glass of water if they are high
½ glass of orange juice if low
½ glass of whole milk if just right or starving

Calories: 680 Total Carb: 55 g

Stir-fried Chicken with Rice: If you keep chicken tenders in your freezer, you can make this meal in 20 minutes. My kids never seem to tire of eating stir-fry.

1 lb chicken
1 Tbsp canola oil
$^1/_2$ cup green onions, chopped
1 cup pea pods
4 cups cooked rice
optional: bean sprouts, cabbage, carrots, and celery

1. Prepare rice.
2. Chop chicken and stir-fry in wok with a dollop of oil until done, (3 or 4 minutes). At this point, I remove the chicken, so it doesn't get tough. Sauté chopped green onions for a minute, then add pod peas. Return chicken to pan. (Add a little soy sauce if your kids like it.) Serve over rice.

Calories: 409 Total Carb: 47 g

You serve up the portions, so you can adjust the carbohydrate (the rice) to your child's needs. You can precook the rice, let it cool, and add all of it to the chicken and vegetables. Make a little ditch in the middle of the rice/chicken and add a raw egg. Stir the egg into the mixture in the pan, and you have another delicious variation to chicken stir-fry.

Stir-fried Beef with Rice or Potatoes: If you have round steak in your freezer and rice or potatoes in your pantry, this meal takes about 20 minutes.

1 lb round steak
1 Tbsp canola oil
1 lb potatoes, peeled then cooked
2 Tbsp butter
$^1/_2$ cup green onions, chopped
Broccoli, optional

1. Chop the steak into small cubes, stir-fry in a small amount of oil until done. Add green onions for a minute.
2. In the meantime, chop potatoes and sauté in butter until tender. Serve stir-fried beef next to the potatoes or mix them together. If your kids like cheese, you can melt Jack cheese over the top. Add a salad, and it's a meal.

Calories: 301 Total Carb: 18 g

The other option is to prepare rice. Stir-fry the steak until done, add the green onions and broccoli pieces and cook until tender. Serve steak and broccoli over rice. Serve with a green salad, or for little folks, carrot sticks and celery.

Beef Stroganoff: This is very easy to make and again is fast if you have steak in the freezer and a can of cream of mushroom soup handy. Serve over noodles with a salad. Serves 4.

1 lb chuck or round steak, cut in bite-sized strips
2 Tbsp butter or olive oil
1 small onion, chopped
1 clove garlic, chopped
Salt and pepper
1 can cream of mushroom soup
Sour cream, optional
4 cups egg noodles

1. Prepare noodles.
2. Brown meat, onion, and garlic in butter over low heat, 20 min. Add soup, salt, and pepper to taste. Cover and simmer over very low heat 30 min. (If your kids like it, add sour cream, up to ½ cup.) Serve over hot drained noodles.

Calories: 481 Total Carb: 48 g

DATE_____   M T W T F S S   *NAME*_____

| Before Break. | | After Break. | | Before Lunch | | After Lunch | | Before Supper | | After Supper | | Bed Time | | Other | |

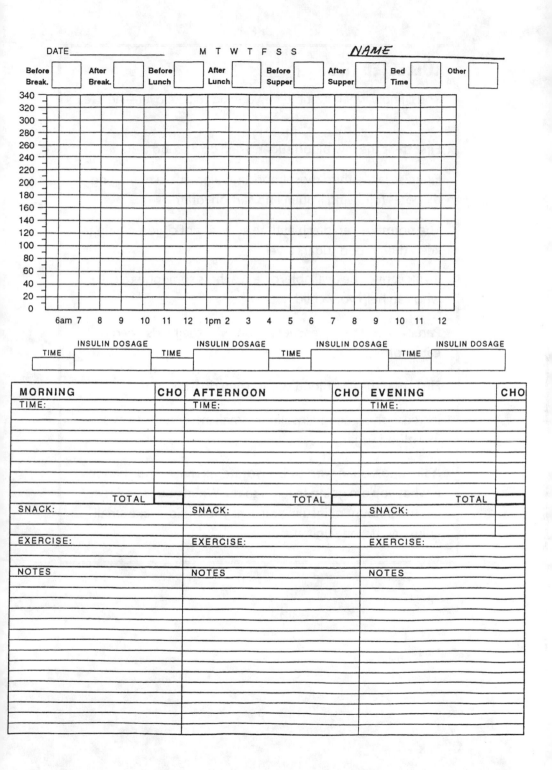

340
320
300
280
260
240
220
200
180
160
140
120
100
80
60
40
20
0
    6am 7   8   9   10 11 12 1pm 2   3   4   5   6   7   8   9   10 11 12

| TIME | INSULIN DOSAGE | TIME | INSULIN DOSAGE | TIME | INSULIN DOSAGE | TIME | INSULIN DOSAGE |

MORNING	CHO	AFTERNOON	CHO	EVENING	CHO
TIME:		TIME:		TIME:	
TOTAL		TOTAL		TOTAL	
SNACK:		SNACK:		SNACK:	
EXERCISE:		EXERCISE:		EXERCISE:	
NOTES		NOTES		NOTES	

COLLECTED TIPS

You'll know when it's time for your kid to take over—he'll tell you.

First treat the low blood sugar. Then do a blood test.

Exercise is the third most important element in managing diabetes following insulin and carbohydrate.

The normal, everyday playtime activities of children help to keep their blood sugars level.

If you cannot be available, give teachers someone to call who can help your child.

Parents need to let teachers know why their kids need to eat so often.

First treat the low blood sugar. Then do a blood test.

Increase short-acting insulin by small increments to avoid low blood sugar.

Adjusting insulin with carbohydrate, exercise, and change is what you are going to learn to do. When you are adjusting the amount of insulin you give your child, make small adjustments, one unit at a time.

Index

About the American Diabetes Association

The American Diabetes Association is the nation's leading voluntary health organization supporting diabetes research, information, and advocacy. Its mission is to prevent and cure diabetes and to improve the lives of all people affected by diabetes. The American Diabetes Association is the leading publisher of comprehensive diabetes information. Its huge library of practical and authoritative books for people with diabetes covers every aspect of self-care—cooking and nutrition, fitness, weight control, medications, complications, emotional issues, and general self-care.

To order American Diabetes Association books: Call 1-800-232-6733. Or log on to http://store.diabetes.org (Do not use www when typing in the web address.)

To join the American Diabetes Association: Call 1-800-806-7801. www.diabetes.org/membership

For more information about diabetes or ADA programs and services: Call 1-800-342-2383. E-mail: Customerservice@diabetes.org or log on to www.diabetes.org

To locate an ADA/NCQA Recognized Provider of quality diabetes care in your area: Call 1-703-549-1500 ext. 2202. www.diabetes.org/recognition/Physicians/ListAll.asp

To find an ADA Recognized Education Program in your area: Call 1-888-232-0822. www.diabetes.org/recognition/education.asp

To join the fight to increase funding for diabetes research, end discrimination, and improve insurance coverage: Call 1-800-342-2383. www.diabetes.org/advocacy

To find out how you can get involved with the programs in your community: Call 1-800-342-2383. See below for program Web addresses.

- *American Diabetes Month:* Educational activities aimed at those diagnosed with diabetes—month of November. www.diabetes.org/ADM
- *American Diabetes Alert:* Annual public awareness campaign to find the undiagnosed—held the fourth Tuesday in March. www.diabetes.org/alert
- *The Diabetes Assistance & Resources Program (DAR):* diabetes awareness program targeted to the Latino community. www.diabetes.org/DAR
- *African American Program:* diabetes awareness program targeted to the African American community. www.diabetes.org/africanamerican
- *Awakening the Spirit: Pathways to Diabetes Prevention & Control:* diabetes awareness program targeted to the Native American community. www.diabetes.org/awakening

To find out about an important research project regarding type 2 diabetes: www.diabetes.org/ada/research.asp

To obtain information on making a planned gift or charitable bequest: Call 1-888-700-7029. www.diabetes.org/ada/plan.asp

To make a donation or memorial contribution: Call 1-800-342-2383. www.diabetes.org/ada/cont.asp